Reexamining World Literature

Serrano calls for a reassessment of the practice of World Literature with six case studies taken from the Arabic, Chinese, French, German, Korean and Latin American traditions. Although in recent years the field has adopted more inclusive and wide-ranging criteria for college-level anthologies of World Literature, and has seen the collection and publication of critical readers, book-length introductions, and even a history, the theoretical predisposition of most of its practitioners paradoxically has led to a shrinking of its horizons and a narrowing of its vision. *Reexamining World Literature* asks scholars to look beyond the current dominant definition of World Literature (works in English with broad reach or works in other languages with significant circulation in English translation) in order to engage with a range of complex texts that elude the field's assumptions. World Literature need not be a we-are-the-world of shared values, but instead should ask readers to question what those values are.

Richard Serrano is Professor of French and Comparative Literature at Rutgers University. His primary research interest is intercultural transmission.

Reexamining World Literature
Challenging Current Assumptions and Envisioning Possibilities

Richard Serrano

NEW YORK AND LONDON

First published 2020
by Routledge
52 Vanderbilt Avenue, New York, NY 10017

and by Routledge
2 Park Square, Milton Park, Abingdon, Oxon, OX14 4RN

Routledge is an imprint of the Taylor & Francis Group, an informa business

© 2020 Taylor & Francis

The right of Richard Serrano to be identified as author of this work has been asserted by him in accordance with sections 77 and 78 of the Copyright, Designs and Patents Act 1988.

All rights reserved. No part of this book may be reprinted or reproduced or utilised in any form or by any electronic, mechanical, or other means, now known or hereafter invented, including photocopying and recording, or in any information storage or retrieval system, without permission in writing from the publishers.

Trademark notice: Product or corporate names may be trademarks or registered trademarks, and are used only for identification and explanation without intent to infringe.

Library of Congress Cataloging-in-Publication Data
A catalog record for this title has been requested

ISBN: 9780367261344 (hbk)
ISBN: 9780367903497 (ebk)

Typeset in Times New Roman
by codeMantra

for Bernadette

Contents

Acknowledgments		viii
Introduction		1
1	Sun Yunfeng (1764–1814): Woman out of Place	5
2	Paul Claudel (1868–1955): Lost before Translation	25
3	Esteban Echeverría (1805–1851): *La Cautiva* Lost to History	45
4	Jamīl Buthayna (7th c.) in the *Book of Songs* (10th c.): Man out of Poetry	61
5	Friedrich Rückert's (1788–1866) *Unnachahmlich* Qur'ān	77
6	Yi Ok (1760–1815): Man out of Time	93
	Conclusion	115
	Bibliography	121
	Index	125

Acknowledgments

I am grateful to Barry Qualls for admonishing me to finish this book and persist in finding a publisher. Thank you to my colleagues in Comparative Literature, Steve Walker and Janet Walker, for recommending that I send the manuscript to Routledge. Without my many patient language teachers in Korea, Argentina, Peru, Colombia, Mexico, France, Germany, Austria, China and Taiwan, I could not have begun to imagine, let alone write, this book. *Reexamining World Literature* is dedicated to Bernadette Cailler, who has been my intellectual *camarade* for over two decades.

Introduction

In this book — or perhaps better put, *with* this book, — I call for a reexamination of the practice of World Literature, a reassessment of its assumptions and a recasting of its vision. Although in recent years the practitioners of World Literature have spurred the revision of college-level anthologies so that they are more inclusive and wide-ranging, and although World Literature's rapid development as a field of inquiry in dialog with Comparative Literature and other fields has achieved a critical mass leading to the collection and publication of readers, book-length introductions and even a history, their predisposition toward theoretical concerns grounded in a relatively small plot of thought rather than the practice of reading has led, oddly, to a shrinking of the field's horizons and a narrowing of its vision. This book encourages scholars to look beyond the sorts of literary works that have ended up in anthologies in order to engage more fully with a vast range of complex texts that do not easily fit into the paradigms of literary and extra-literary value dominating the field. We should not accept current definitions of World Literature (which is, essentially, works in English with broad reach or works in other languages with significant circulation in English translation), but instead seek out those works that call into question our assumptions about what World Literature can be and then make them available to readers who otherwise will not have access to them.

It may seem at times that I criticize unduly the field of World Literature and its practitioners. Whatever criticism I offer does not rise from disdain or antipathy, but instead marks a sharp-elbowed engagement with scholarship I consider vital. I do feel very strongly, even passionately, that we scholars of World Literature need to work past our own limits and limitations. While it is true that no one scholar can know everything, we can know *something* and can choose to a large degree to push at the boundaries of what we know.

2 Introduction

This book aims to take a close look at what's been overlooked, to think hard about what yet-unspoken assumptions about what we should read cause us to miss engagement with authors who somehow don't quite fit within the parameters of World Literature. An ever-narrowing field asking the same questions of the same works over and over already surrenders to loss, the loss of a knowing, of a perspective, of an unimagined way of organizing experience of the world because a work is beyond one's individual reach.

Comparative Literature, of which I consider World Literature a kissing cousin, is not a shortcut to understanding, a magic formula to making sense of what eludes us. Several years ago a graduate student in Comparative Literature came to my office to ask me which article by Gayatri Spivak she should read in order to analyze a book by Assia Djebbar. I asked her to let me think about this over the weekend. The following Monday I sent her a brief bibliography of literary criticism and historical background related to Algerian Literature and suggested half a dozen other Algerian writers of French expression she might read in order to better place Djebbar within her own tradition. Needless to say, I did not receive a reply and, indeed, never heard from this student again. Perhaps she went on to write a brilliant article about Assia Djebbar; I never bothered to check and as I write this sentence I am not moved to do so. It struck me then that it was not my job to shepherd students and scholars into thinking a certain way about a writer that at that moment was the default for Francophone Literature scholarship — who didn't have an article about Djebbar in those days? Maybe, I thought, this student should read something else. And maybe this student should read something else in a way not merely aping another scholar.

This book suggests, gingerly and respectfully I hope, that we could all benefit from reading something else. Maybe we should read the obscure eighteenth-century Chinese woman poet rather than the celebrated eighteenth-century Chinese novel (or: in addition to). Maybe we should read the Japanese poet mocking the French poet Paul Claudel. Maybe we should read the execrable nineteenth-century wanna-be epic Argentine poem. Maybe we should read the tenth-century narratives into which putatively seventh-century lines of Arabic poetry have been embedded (rather than merely extracting the verse and discarding the prose like so much Amazon packaging). Maybe we should read a German verse translation of the Qur'ān that aims to match the original's beauty. Maybe we should read the Korean poet that even Koreans require translation to understand. Maybe instead of suggesting Algerian

Introduction 3

History and Algerian writers to the graduate student years ago, I should have told her to read Sun Yunfeng, Nagano Shigeharu, Esteban Echeverría, al-Iṣfahānī, Friedrich Rückert and Yi Ok. Perhaps we should read not what everyone else has read, and not use the same tired and worn-out theoretical perspectives, but instead what almost no one we know has read.

This book is about just those works that remain beyond the ken of the World Lit crowd. It not only explores these authors largely ignored, but also considers what it means that they are unread and how overlooking them and looking past them distorts the field of World Literature. Although it is impossible to avoid all cultural biases in the selection of works deemed valuable enough — the determination of value can only be culturally specific — to enter the domain of World Literature, it is nonetheless incumbent upon scholars to be aware of the biases that facilitate or block the awareness of works, authors and entire literatures. This book points out that works that demand extensive contextualization, especially within a tradition or overlapping traditions with their own norms and standards that do not mesh well with ours, are liable to be omitted. Texts that resist ideological modes of reading that have become fashionable over the past fifty years may be excluded in favor of works that serve as fodder for Theory-bound or politically motivated argument. Scholars should not automatically exclude works that get it wrong from an ideological perspective that may be outdated in twenty years anyway. Eventually all authors get it wrong as the years, decades and centuries roll on, assigning value to *connaissance* that prevents *savoir*, two distinct kinds of knowledge that the English language does not recognize. Scholars need to be vigilant about the disappearing text. They need to be wary of ignoring or pushing aside works that do not fit into familiar genre boundaries. Finally, scholars need to recognize World Literature as home to authors with nowhere else to go.

World Literature is not new. Nor is it Western à la Goethe. There have been and still are other worlds of literature. French-reading and German-reading readers have access to works that monolingual English-reading readers do not, for no other reason that these works exist in French and German (and Japanese, and Bahasa Indonesia, and Russian, etc.) translation and not yet in English. While World Literature is clearly an anglophone and largely U.S. endeavor, it does not mean we should not recognize that there are literary works circulating elsewhere in other languages. For centuries Arabic-language works circulated from Western Africa to

4 *Introduction*

the Indian subcontinent and well beyond; it was already a World Literature of vast reach. Similarly, readers in Japan, Korea, Taiwan and Vietnam (and beyond) were so deeply influenced by Chinese culture that, although they spoke different languages, they nonetheless shared a common writing system and espoused variations of a set of values represented in the works circulating among them. This, too, was a World Literature of vast reach.

Generalization and theorization are inevitable; it is difficult to make sense of anything without some recourse to both. However, generalization and theorization should not replace the specific and the particular, but instead spring from them. What most alarms me about World Literature is the disappearance of the text, as if scholars are undergraduates who not only don't do the reading, but also can't imagine why they would be expected to do it. With this book I read works of literature and extract generalizations from them while, I hope, never straying so far from the read text that we forget its existence. There are no doubt scholars who will disagree with or even dislike the way I read, but I hope that they will appreciate the opportunity to get a look at what I have read that they may have not.

1 Sun Yunfeng (1764–1814)
Woman out of Place

In his introduction to *What Is World Literature?* David Damrosch suggests that some hapless works of literature may find themselves appearing and disappearing from the coveted category:

> A given work can enter into world literature and then fall out of it again if it shifts beyond a threshold point along either axis, the literary or the worldly. Over the centuries an unusually shifty work can come in and out of the sphere of world literature several different times. (6)

Although one might suspect that Damrosch is accusing one work or another of duplicity in its endeavor to enter World Literature, I suppose that by shifty here he means texts that shift out of sight along the literary or worldly axes. It does, however, feel as if Damrosch very nearly assigns consciousness to literary works as they compete for sufficiently worldly literatureness. In part this is because he wants scholars to understand literature as a marketplace of sorts; our task then is to trace shadows of the invisible hand that pushes individual texts this or that way along these axes. Even while he performs complex, thrilling readings of literary works from the four corners of the world and beyond, Damrosch never lays out clear criteria for determining where along these two axes a text might disappear just beyond the horizon. When can it no longer be seen? And from whose perspective might it slip from view? In this chapter I try to determine whether the poetry of 孫雲鳳 Sun Yunfeng, a Chinese woman from the long eighteenth century (another horizon stretched, not only chronologically, but geographically, from Western Europe to East Asia), is shifty enough to be espied, on occasion, from a Damroschian tower.

Perhaps the first question to ask is not whether Sun Yunfeng has entered World Literature, but whether she has entered *Chinese*

6 Sun Yunfeng

Literature. Although writers or their works can inhabit spaces of intersection between a category of a particular national literature and World Literature (with national literature as a category not terribly helpful in many instances — there is no actual Arabia into which Arabic Literature may be conveniently tossed, for example, and no Francophonia to house Francophone Literature), there are examples of texts that seem to enter World Literature first and then are only grudgingly admitted into the category of literature within their own linguistic traditions. *1001 Nights* is a famous example of a work first recognized as literature in French and English translation and then, as it becomes ever more emblematic of Arab culture in Europe and North America, embraced reluctantly by Arab scholars as literature as well. The *Qur'ān*, as I will discuss in a later chapter, may have entered World Literature as literature particularly well-suited to diversify a World Literature anthology's readings beyond the West and before the twentieth century, but few Arab Muslims are comfortable reading it as they might read *Huckleberry Finn* or, more to the point, considering its difficulty without extensive exegesis, *Finnegans Wake*. In other words, a work may leap straight into World Literature without ever actually having passed through a category of national or a group of national literatures bound by a common language.

If anthologization is a sign of a writer's arrival, then Sun Yunfeng qualifies for figuring prominently in 袁枚 Yuan Mei's 隨園女弟子詩選 *Anthology of Poetry by the Female Disciples of Harmony Garden* (1796). Yuan Mei (1716–1797), generally agreed to be the most important Chinese poet of the eighteenth century, endorsed and nurtured the composition of poetry by Sun Yunfeng and other women poets, several of whom became his 弟子, a word that can be translated disciple (as above), follower or student, although the women whose poetry he praised and promoted were never quite any of these things. In the last few years of his long life he corresponded with several women poets from the gentry class in Jiangnan, the wealthy and productive region of China just south of the Yangtze River, and took part in three day-long gatherings with them in Hangzhou and Suzhou. Yuan Mei had a well-earned reputation for eccentricity, for in addition to supporting women's poetry and education he also compiled ghost stories and recipes and was known for his variable sexual preferences. His predilection for women poets did not go uncriticized during his lifetime and after his death, but it is likely that the unhappy experiences of his talented sisters, neither of whom was ever able to fully realize her talents, played a greater part in his decision to encourage women poets than his eccentricities or peccadilloes.

Despite the vast numbers of Chinese women who composed and published poetry during the Qing (1644–1911), as recently as 1982 a history of the development of Chinese poetry nearly 1400 pages long could find space to mention only five women poets, "none of them from periods later than the Song Dynasty" (960–1279) (Robertson, 64). Indeed, it is likely that more poetry was written by Chinese women in the eighteenth century than in the twentieth (Schmidt, 2008, 130). It would be tempting then to blame the disappearance of Sun Yunfeng and other late imperial women poets from literary history on mere sexism, but the vagaries of how scholars writing in the twentieth-century periodized literature by genre were in part responsible. According to this schema, the genre of novel best represented Qing Literature, just as drama best represented Yuan (1271–1368) Literature, with poetry emblematic of the Tang (618–904). This way of shrinking the Chinese canon into manageable categories devalued the poetry of Sun Yunfeng's era, and helped to scrub her name from literary history. It certainly was no boon that the women of Sun Yunfeng's time and social class wrote in traditional forms that within a century of her death came to be considered retrograde and pointless. Sun Yunfeng was celebrated during her lifetime for a poetry that adhered to traditional forms and topics at a time when such adherence was requisite; it was her posthumous misfortune that this adherence would become instead suspect during a century of revolutions, both political and literary.

Sun Yunfeng's return from beyond the threshold back into the history of Chinese Literature depends not on Yuan Mei, long dead, or any other Chinese patron, but instead on the literary archeology performed by feminist criticism that has also returned attention, through anthologies, reading lists and monographs, to eighteenth-century European women writers. To a large degree, then, Sun Yunfeng's place in Chinese Literature, if she has one, is due not to her own shiftiness, but to the shiftiness of scholars beyond China, scholars who have extended the parameters of their fields of research and thereby returned to view the work of writers that have trundled down one axis or another. Articles, books and conferences by Ellen Widmer, Dorothy Ko, Grace Fong, Susan Mann and others have reinserted Chinese women's poetry into history and literature and grant them an attention perhaps unmatched since Yuan Mei's death at the end of the eighteenth century. Of such stuff is World Literature made and, I suppose, unmade.

Does Sun Yunfeng's return to Chinese Literature through the good offices of scholars based in the United States mean that she

8   *Sun Yunfeng*

has found a place in World Literature? Although several of her poems appear in English translation in what is to date the most extensive anthology of pre-twentieth-century Chinese women's writing in English, *Women Writers of Traditional China: An Anthology of Poetry and Criticism* (1999), she has garnered only scattered mention in criticism that prefers to focus on other writers.[1] Unlike 屈秉筠 Qu Bingyun, another of Yuan Mei's disciples, Sun Yunfeng has not succeeded in inspiring a monograph of her own. Nor does she appear in any of the anthologies of World Literature. Damrosch's *Longman Anthology* gives the eighteenth-century East Asian slot to 紅樓夢 *Dream of the Red Chamber* (under the alternate title *Story of the Stone*, which its translator David Hawkes preferred), as does the *Norton Anthology of World Literature*. Cao Xueqin's phenomenal novel certainly deserves to be read, although the choice reinforces the traditional Chinese division of genres by dynasty. Despite its great length (or perhaps because of it) *Dream of the Red Chamber* is more easily presented to the World Literature reader than the poetry of Sun Yunfeng and her cohort. Although part of a rich tradition of vernacular fiction, Cao Xueqin's novel is so astonishing as to be virtually *sui generis. Dream of the Red Chamber* creates its own world; part of the novel's point is that its characters are hermetically sealed within it and unable to escape. Although a knowledge of other Chinese novels and Chinese history would not impede the work of the reader, he need not leave the world created by the novel either. Reading *Dream of the Red Chamber* demands immersion; the great pleasure of the text is losing oneself in another world.

Sun Yunfeng's poems, however, depend on the vast reaches of the Chinese lyric tradition in order to hang significance on their brief and slender frameworks. Her poems, like most classical Chinese poems, force the reader to think well beyond them in order to plumb their depths. Although deceptively simple to read and translate, they are embedded in sub-genres of poetry with long and complex histories. It is the friction between the details of her poems and the expectations of these sub-genres established over centuries or millennia that generate meaning. They do not lend themselves to easy explication by or for the World Literature reader. I would also argue that their inability to meet the expectations of the scholar reading them as a woman's poetry has further marginalized them. Two decades after resurfacing, Sun Yunfeng remains largely unread. In the rest of this chapter I will explore the challenges and potential disappointments of her poetry that seem to shift her further and further away along the axes of World Literature.

Sun Yunfeng's life is unusual enough for her time and social class to merit a brief biography.[2] When she was seven years old one of her father's guests challenged her by reciting the first line of the first poem of the 詩經 *Classic of Poetry*, the foundation of Chinese poetry and a book all Chinese civil examination candidates were required to learn. Rather than replying with the second line of the famous poem, as expected, she instead recited a parallel line on the same theme from another poem in the same collection. This demonstrated that she was precocious, erudite and spirited. Her father, a wealthy government functionary, encouraged her and her two younger sisters to compose poetry. After her father introduced her to Yuan Mei's poetry in her early twenties, she took it upon herself to send him a poem that used the same rhymes as one that the master had composed upon leaving West Lake in Hangzhou. As a result she became Yuan Mei's first female disciple. In 1790 he held his first of three gatherings with thirteen of his female disciples (although only ten names are given in his account) when he returned to West Lake to sweep the graves of his ancestors. The two gatherings that took place in Hangzhou were held at the villa of the Sun family, reinforcing the notion that Sun Yunfeng was among his favorites. At this gathering poetry was recited and discussed, a banquet was enjoyed and a couple of famous male poets joined them at one point. Beyond these details about her life as a poet, Sun Yunfeng was said to often accompany her father on his official travels, and she was married to the poet 程庭懋 Cheng Tingmao, although her reputation seems to have eclipsed his, since I have found no trace of his poetry. Although her upbringing was privileged and her father enlightened about the education of women, she was by no means unique. By the beginning of the eighteenth century many women among the nobility were not only literate but were also writing, exchanging and publishing their poetry.

Since Sun Yunfeng's poems are not annotated or dated, it is difficult to pinpoint when or where she composed them or to what end, which means that some of their ambiguity results from decontextualization. This matters because classical Chinese poetry was usually occasional — and indeed there are references in Yuan Mei's collected works to lines of poetry she composed in letters to him or at one of his poetry gatherings in Hangzhou. Nonetheless, even those poems whose occasion is unknown are not difficult to categorize by sub-genre, which makes it possible to speculate on how a Chinese reader's expectations were satisfied or thwarted. I will look at two types of poems that she composed, boudoir poems and

10   *Sun Yunfeng*

travel poems, both of which are closely identified with male poets, but for different reasons. Because travel was still largely restricted to men at the end of the eighteenth century, only a handful of women had the opportunity to write travel poetry (although some travel poetry by women was about imaginary journeys, divided into two categories, 臥遊 recumbent travel and 遊仙 roaming as a transcendent [Wang, 3, 31]). Indeed, for the nobility movement beyond the threshold of the home itself was generally limited to men. As for the boudoir complaint or boudoir lament 閨怨, it was a short poem nearly always written by a man in the voice of a woman or about a woman alone in her room longing for the absent man, often because he has failed to keep a rendezvous. It might seem strange to restrict such a genre to male poets, but it was understood that the poet assumed the position of a woman in this situation as an allegory for his role as supplicant to the emperor or a powerful minister who ignored him. As the boudoir complaint persisted over the centuries, its purpose seems to have become primarily competitive — who could write the most heart-wrenching poem in as few words as possible all the while cramming it with references to the sorts of objects a woman prohibited from stepping out of the palace would surround herself with to console her loneliness.

Since Sun Yunfeng chose to write in sub-genres of poetry that are highly gender-inflected, does that mean she was trying to say something about what it meant to be a woman at the end of the eighteenth century? In the case of the boudoir complaint, was her lyric persona a woman pretending to be a man pretending to be a woman? Or did she, by speaking in this voice, make the woman a veritable woman, stripping the poems of allegory? Do her travel poems reflect on what it means to be a woman traveler or does she assume an apparently gender-neutral voice, which would then represent the unfettered man's access to travel? The examples that follow represent seven of her twenty-nine poems anthologized by Yuan Mei in 1796. All the translations are mine. Because certain aspects of classical Chinese poetry are especially difficult to render into English, I have chosen not to rhyme the lines (since the language has continued to evolve since the eighteenth century, the rhymes are not always evident when pronounced in today's standard Chinese anyway). Nor have I made any attempt to account for the complex manipulation of tones that are an important part of classical Chinese poetry. Instead I have focused on translating the imagery and reproducing the parallelism within the couplets. The numbers in parentheses following the Chinese text indicate the page on which it is found in Yuan Mei's *Anthology of Poetry by the Female Disciples of Harmony Garden*.

Although Sun Yunfeng does not always refrain from using subject markers in her poems, this first poem is entirely free of pronouns, which is usually the case in classical Chinese poetry. The "I" and "we" of the translations are additions so that the poem makes sense in English. "Traveler" 客 in the last line of the poem is probably a reference to the speaker of the poem, a way of emphasizing that she (if indeed the speaker is to be understood as a woman) is far from home.

舟中度歲

連朝風不定,
守歲泊江船.
遠水落殘照,
孤城生暮烟.
凍雲催淑氣,
鄉思入新年.
杯少屠酥味,
村醪點客筵. (23)

Passing into the New Year on a Boat

Day after day the wind's been uncertain,
So we observe the New Year on a boat anchored in the river.
Far across the water what's left of the light sets;
The isolated city gives way to dusk haze.
Frozen clouds rush the warm air;
I long for home as we enter the new year.
There aren't enough cups — the reek of *tusu*;
Village liquor is spilled on the traveler's bamboo mat.

The building block of this sort of classical Chinese poem is the couplet. This poem is constructed of four. Each couplet provides a snapshot that brings the reader ever closer to the traveler. The first couplet represents a boat anchored in the river, seen from beyond the gaze of the speaker. The second couplet aligns the reader's gaze with that of the speaker. The third couplet invites the reader into the mind of the speaker. And the fourth couplet ends the poem by directing attention to the poor rural substitute for the *tusu* liquor used to ring in the new year. There are not enough cups to go around, so all she gets is what is spilled on her bamboo mat. Bringing the reader ever closer to the speaker only emphasizes her loneliness.

12 *Sun Yunfeng*

What is unusual about this poem, within the context of Qing women's travel poetry, is its resolute refusal to indicate clearly that the speaker is a woman. Yanning Wang's recent survey of Qing travel poetry written by women presents example after example in which the poet links the text to her specific, gendered experience. A woman might travel in order to follow her father, husband or son assigned to administer a town in a different part of the empire. Or she might travel in order to return her husband's corpse to his hometown upon his death. Or she might, on the rare occasion, travel in order to visit her parents or other close relatives. All the examples Wang offers are explicitly tied to some event that demands the woman poet go beyond the bounds of her normal lived experience. Travel for any other reason, such as merely to join other women in making a pilgrimage to a temple, risked censure (Wang, 101). Since there are no pronouns or other grammatical markers to indicate the speaker's gender in the original Chinese, that leaves only cultural context. The final couplet of the poem suggests that the traveler is not offered any of the inferior liquor; instead all she gets is a splash of it on her bamboo mat. The travel experiences evoked in these poems often seem incomplete or disappointing. Perhaps it is true that there are not enough cups to go around, but the speaker's denial of *tusu* and the downgrading of her experience of the celebration to spilled booze may be a sign of the restrictions her gender impose on her.

In the next poem the speaker refers to herself with 我, which means "I" or even "we," since in classical Chinese 我 may be singular or plural (modern Chinese distinguishes between 我 "I" and 我們 "we," but classical Chinese does not). "Traveler" in the third line is probably self-referential, as it was in the last poem.

征程

春来江上雁知还,
我尚驱车歧路间.
芳草极天迷客思,
白云何处是乡关.
地卑城郭多临水,
县小人家半住山.
闻说西行多石径,
喜无尘土扑征颜. (24)

Sun Yunfeng 13

A Journey

Springtime I arrive at the river's edge — the wild goose would
 know to return,
But I still drive the carriage between the branching paths.
The sweet smell of grass reaches heaven, confounding the
 traveler's thoughts,
White clouds — where is the pass to the village?
Cities of the earth are below — many at water's edge;
The country folk live half way up the mountain.
I've heard that traveling west there are many stone paths;
I'm happy that no dust will be cast in my face by the journey.

The first couplet mentions a choice made to continue traveling
although it might not be a good idea. The second couplet joins the
intensity of the experience to the result of the decision to travel
on — the traveler is lost. In the third couplet the traveler pauses to
take in the scene. In the final couplet the traveler imagines that the
rest of the journey will be easier ("no dust"). Unless the reader believes that the speaker of the poem is literally driving the carriage,
which would strongly suggest that the speaker is a man, since no
woman of Sun Yunfeng's social class would take the reins under
any but the most extreme circumstances, there is no clear indication
of the speaker's gender. The dust in the final line of the poem is a
reminder that heretofore the journey has been difficult. Sun Yunfeng's travel poems are seldom free of impediment to the enjoyment
of the experience.

 In the next poem, Sun Yunfeng not only uses the subject pronoun
我 "I" or "we," but begins the poem with "traveler" 客, which also
refers to the speaker of the poem. The poem begins then with an
assertion of the poem's subjectivity.

山行

客思西風裏,
車塵暮靄間.
蟲聲黃葉路,
人影夕陽山.
鳥去一何速,
我行猶未還.
臨溪羨漁者,
幽意獨閑閑. (23)

14 *Sun Yunfeng*

Mountain Journey

A traveler stops to think within the West Wind;
A carriage is dusty within dusk's haze.
The drone of insects on the path strewn with yellow leaves;
Shadows of people on the mountain facing the setting sun.
A bird flies off quickly;
I walk as if never to return.
At stream's edge I envy someone fishing,
Secluded thought, solitude and repose.

In the first couplet, as in the previous poem, the dusty carriage suggests the discomfort of the voyage. That the carriage stops (probably *must* stop) when the sun sets may indicate that the traveler has lost her way or at least has not yet reached her destination. The West Wind is generally associated with autumn, reinforced here by the yellow leaves in the second couplet. The year's end is quick approaching, as is the end of the day. In the third couplet, the traveler is again contrasted with a bird that makes a different choice or has a different option. The final couplet introduces a stock figure from Chinese landscape poetry, the enviable fisherman who need only spend his day quietly. If the traveler is understood to be a woman, then longing to be a man sitting alone with his fishing pole is all the more poignant, although, strictly speaking, no gender is assigned to the "someone" fishing either.

The final two travel poems evoke pilgrimage to a temple. In the first poem the reference to a bell makes this clear.

曉行

殘月曉霜鐘,
馬蹄黃葉路.
日出不見人,
溪聲隔烟樹. (19)

Dawn Walk

Waning moon — morning frost on a bell;
Horse hooves — yellow leaves on a road.
The sun rises with no one to be seen;
A creek murmurs beyond mist and trees. (p.19)

The first couplet is a perfect example of parallelism, with each character in the second line matching the function of that in the first line, which I have tried to reproduce in the translation. Either the chill of the morning or the sound of a horse's hooves, or both, has disturbed the speaker's sleep. In the second couplet her senses heightened by the absence of other people (not yet awake?) allow her to hear a brook that she cannot see. There are no pronouns and no indication whatsoever of the speaker's gender here. The experience has been rendered universal.

These three poems are accomplished and moving, capturing a state of mind induced by encounters with the world made possible by travel. What a World Literature reader misses and what my analysis so far has avoided mentioning is that Sun Yunfeng is in dialog with an extraordinarily long and rich tradition of travel poetry. I include below two poems by other, earlier writers simply to demonstrate that the elements Sun Yunfeng uses to construct the world of these poems are all to be found in the work of her predecessors. I do not mean to suggest that she was necessarily influenced by these two poems in particular, but that the stone paths, boats, fishermen, creeks, mists, forests, and so on enter her poem not from the real world through which the poet traveled, but are instead props already found on the stage of Chinese travel poetry for well over a millennium. The first example is from Qiwu Qian (early eighth century), about whom little is known, while the second example is by Du Mu (803–852), a famous poet of the late Tang (http://ctext.org/text.pl?node=130889&if=en, http://ctext.org/dictionary.pl?if=en&id=211496).[3]

綦毋潛 春泛若耶溪

幽意無斷絕
此去隨所偶.
晚風吹行舟,
花路入溪口.
際夜轉西壑,
隔山望南斗.
潭煙飛溶溶,
林月低向後.
生事且彌漫,
願為持竿叟.

Floating on Ruoye Creek in Spring (by Qiwu Qian)

Secluded thought without end,
On this trip I follow whatever's encountered;
The evening breeze blows the boat down

16 *Sun Yunfeng*

A blossom path into the creek's mouth;
At the edge of night I turn into West Pool,
Beyond the mountains I gaze at the Southern Dipper;
The mist over the pools hovers;
The forest moon sets behind me.
Life's worries still fill the air;
If only I were an old man holding a fishing pole.

杜牧 山行

遠上寒山石徑斜
白雲生處有人家
停車坐愛楓林晚
霜葉紅於二月花

Mountain Journey (by Du Mu)

Far away on the cold mountain are steep stone paths
White clouds give way to a place where people make their home.
I stop the carriage and just sit, for I love the maple forest in
   the evening,
Frost-laden leaves are redder than February's blossoms.

What these poems composed by men, which I have chosen more
or less at random from the extant thousands like them, seem to
lack that is found in Sun Yunfeng's similarly themed poems is a
sense of the difficulty of the journey. Perhaps therein is gender
found.

The final travel poem by Sun Yunfeng I present is more complex.
It evokes a visit to a famous temple on a mountain just west of West
Lake near Hangzhou, which is where Sun Yunfeng spent her adult
life.

登韜光寺

靈鷲峰頭寺,
清幽少俗氛.
竹深人不見,
木落鳥成群.
海氣蒸紅日,
山泉瀉白雲.
我來游未足,
莫遣暮鐘聞. (23)

Ascent to the Temple of Concealed Brilliance

There is a temple on the summit of Vulture Peak
Where clarity and seclusion dissipate the world's miasma.
The bamboo is thick and no one is seen,
A tree falls and birds form flocks.
Sea fog rises to turn the sun red;
A mountain spring courses into white clouds.
I have come but the journey is incomplete;
Do not send me away before I hear the bell at dusk.

The Temple of Concealed Brilliance was named after a Buddhist monk from Sichuan who lived alone in a hut on the peak where the current temple is located. When he was governor of Hangzhou the famed poet 白居易 Bo Juyi (772–846) became his friend and exchanged poems with him. Vulture Peak in the first couplet is the name of a mountain in India to which Buddha often retreated. It was believed to have been magically transported to West Lake, where it took the name 飛來峰, "The Peak that Flew Hither." The third and fourth couplets evoke a series of cause-and-effect. The bamboo is so thick that no one can be seen. When a tree falls, birds fly off in a flock. When fog rises from the ocean it turns the sun red. A mountain spring seems to end in white clouds. Each line gives way to another in which the effect is less real than apparent; the sun is not *really* red, nor does the mountain spring truly turn into clouds. In the last couplet the sudden intrusion of the first-person 我 comes as a shock after three couplets of landscape without people and without any self-reference.

Stranger yet is that the poem ends with an interrupted experience, or at the very least seems to end with a plea that the experience be allowed to continue. The poem ends without a response. This is not how a trip to a temple atop a mountain is supposed to turn out. Bo Juyi records his much more typical experience more than a thousand years earlier at a temple southwest of Chang'an, the then capital of Tang China (http://ctext.org/text.pl?node=189024&if=en).

仙游寺獨宿 (白居易)

沙鶴上階立, 潭月當戶開。
此中留我宿, 兩夜不能回。
幸與靜境遇, 喜無歸侶催。
從今獨遊后, 不擬共人來。

18 *Sun Yunfeng*

Lodging Alone at Transcendent Journey Temple (by Bo Juyi)

The sand crane is at the top of the stairs;
The pond moon is just at the open door.
Between them I make my bed;
For two nights I could not turn away.
I'm lucky to have come across a place so still;
I'm glad to have no companion who'd nag me to leave.
From this lone journey on
I'll never bring someone along.

Although I have felt compelled to insert "I" into the translation, there are in fact no pronouns in the poem. The speaker of the poem seems to take advantage of the solitude in this abandoned place to disappear into the scene. After reading Sun Yunfeng's poem one might understand why Bo Juyi would vow to always thereafter overnight at temples alone, with only a reflected moon and a large bird to keep him company. It is difficult to imagine someone telling Bo Juyi, 杜甫 Du Fu (712–770), 李白 Li Bo (701–762), or any of the famous poets of the Chinese tradition, "Time's up!" The speaker of Sun Yunfeng's poem seems to be addressing someone with the authority to compel her departure before the pilgrimage has come to a satisfying conclusion. A close look at Sun Yunfeng's travel poetry finds spilt booze, getting lost, envy of other's solitude, lots of dust, paths not yet taken and unreached destinations. Transcendence is never attained; the closest she comes is when she snatches a moment before others awaken, but even that brief poem is cut short before she can manage to peer far beyond her own existence.

Reading her boudoir complaints may prove yet more puzzling. Before I turn to them, I present three examples of the genre to give some sense of what it is. The first two examples are by Bo Juyi and Li Bo, among the most famous of China's poets (http://ctext.org/text.pl?node=193279&if=en, http://ctext.org/text.pl?node=140341&if=en).

後宮詞 (白居易)

淚傸羅巾夢不成，
夜深前殿按歌聲。
紅顏未老恩先斷，
斜倚薰籠坐到明。

Song from the Empress's Quarters (by Bo Juyi)

Tears soak her silk handkerchief — her dream is incomplete;
Night deepens before the palace — voices break out in song.
Her pink cheeks are not yet old, but his favor is already cut short.
She slumps against the basket over her incense burner until
    dawn breaks.

怨情 (李白)

美人卷珠帘，
深坐蹙蛾眉。
但見淚痕湿，
不知心恨谁。

Complaining of Love (by Li Bo)

The beautiful woman rolls up her pearl-studded screen,
She sits for ages knitting her moth-brows.
Although the moist traces of her tears can still be seen,
No one knows whom she hates in her heart.

Both poems depict spurned women who suffer in beautiful sur-
roundings. The woman in Bo Juyi's poem has a gauzy silk handkerchief and brazier she uses to burn incense to dry and scent her
clothing, while the woman in Li Bo's poem has a roll-up screen en-
crusted with pearls at her window, as well as meticulously painted
eyebrows.

The third example, by 薛逢 Xue Feng (816-?), a minor poet of
the Tang, takes the basic elements of the boudoir complaint to an
extreme (http://ctext.org/text.pl?node=216915&if=en).

薛逢 宮詞

十二樓中盡曉妝，
望仙樓上望君王。
鎖銜金獸連環冷，
水滴銅龍晝漏長。
雲髻罷梳還對鏡，
羅衣欲換更添香。
遙窺正殿簾開處，
袍袴宮人掃御床。

20 *Sun Yunfeng*

Palace Poem (by Xue Feng)

Within their twelve separate chambers they spend the day
    adorning themselves,
From Gazing-on-the-Transcendent Tower they look out for
    their lord king.
The golden beast lock's door-chains have grown cold,
The bronze dragon water clock drips all day long.
One stops combing her cloud-coils of hair but still faces the
    mirror,
She wants to change her silk garment and add yet more perfume.
From far off she peers between the curtains into the main hall:
Palace servants in uniform sweep the imperial bed-chamber.

Xue Feng's poem is over the top. In the first couplet there is not one
woman waiting but instead twelve. They spend all morning deck-
ing themselves out although their master is away. They seem to expect his imminent return, looking for him from the vantage point
of Gazing-on-the-Transcendent Tower, its name mocking their real
purpose. In the second couplet the decor is elaborate and baroquely
bestial. The chains attached to the lock on the door of their complex have grown cold because there has been no reason to unlock
them. The water clock is a reminder of how slowly time is passing,
one drop at a time. In the third couplet the poem seems to focus on
one of the women, who has stopped combing her hair even as she
continues to peer into her mirror; what she sees makes her want
to change her clothes and reapply perfume. The final couplet reveals what her sharp eyes have seen: uniformed servants in another
building are preparing their master's bed. It seems the waiting will
soon come to an end — but which of the twelve will be chosen?

Sun Yunfeng titles her boudoir complaints 古意 "Ancient Feelings," which suggests that she understood it as an imitation of her
long-ago predecessors.

古意

銀燈結雙蕊,
蟢子上裙帶.
早起洗蹄妝,
凝歡畫長黛. (19)

Ancient Feelings

A silver lamp knots a pair of wicks;
A black spider climbs a woman's sash.

Early she rises to wipe off tear-stained make-up;
Fixing her joy, she paints long black eyebrows.

Although the poem is composed of only two couplets, it contains the grieving woman and material signs of palace life typical of a boudoir complaint. The pair of wicks in the silver lamp are a painful reminder that the woman, in contrast, is unpaired. The spider might seem at first a puzzling visitor, but the word for spider 蟢 *xǐ* contains 喜 *xǐ* happiness. The Chinese word for marital bliss is two happinesses together: 囍, also pronounced *xǐ*. That she has a spider for a visitor instead of her man is bad enough; that she ends up with only one *xǐ* rather than two makes it even worse. The woman in Sun Yunfeng's boudoir complaint seems less despairing than those in either Li Bo or Bo Juyi's, as she rises to apply her mask of make-up. The sash and the spider are not Sun Yunfeng's invention; they also show up in an example from 權德輿 Quan Deyu (759–818) (http://ctext.org/text.pl?node=170662&if=en).

權德輿 玉臺體

昨夜裙帶解，
今朝蟢子飛。
鉛華不可棄，
莫是藁砧歸。

A Poem in the Style of the *Jade Terrace Collection* (by Quan Deyu)

Last night my sash came loose;
This morning the spider flew off.
If I give up make-up I'll end up
Back beating laundry on a rock.

Jade Terrace Collection refers to 玉臺新詠 *New Songs from the Jade Terrace*, a sixth-century anthology of love poetry reaching back as far as the 漢 Han Dynasty (206 BCE–200 CE), with many examples of the boudoir complaint. The resigned tone of Sun Yunfeng's poem falls somewhere between the despair of those by Li Bo and Bo Juyi and the pragmatic attitude expressed by the woman in Quan Deyu's poem.

The final example from Sun Yunfeng is also titled "Ancient Feelings." While it perhaps is not strictly speaking a boudoir complaint, it is nonetheless another poem in which Sun Yunfeng assumes to voice of a certain kind of woman whose experience is distant from her own.

22   *Sun Yunfeng*

古意

庭空月皎蝙蝠飛，
當戶女兒愁鳴機.
投校太息起拜月，
霜色在樹生風衣.
千里盈盈不得語，
捲簾仰望星河稀. (21)

In the empty courtyard the moon is bright — bats fly off;

Facing the door the daughter grieves at the sound of the loom;
She casts aside its shuttle with a heavy sigh and rises to bow to
    the moon;
The color of frost on the trees — the wind gives life to her robes.
A thousand miles and on and on — she cannot gather the words,
Rolls up the screen and looks up at the Star River wearing thin.

The first couplet signals immediately that something is wrong. In classical Chinese poetry the moon is a sign of remembering someone who is far away (because although separated they can look at the same moon), while the second character in the word for bat 蝠 *fú* sounds like 福 *fú*, which means "good fortune." The bats have flown off and so has good fortune, while the girl has stayed behind to weave; it is hard to imagine a more gender-specific task. In the second couplet she abandons her weaving and turns her attention to the world outside her door. In the final couplet she looks far beyond her own world to see the Milky Way.

Sun Yunfeng interweaves allusions to two famous Chinese female figures through this poem. The first obvious allusion is the early seventh-century anonymous 木蘭詩 "Ballad of Mulan" (http:// ctext.org/dictionary.pl).[4] The long poem begins

唧唧復唧唧，
木蘭當戶織。
不聞機杼聲，
惟聞女嘆息。

Click click again click click;
Mulan facing the door weaves.
No one can hear the sound of the shuttle,
All they can hear is the girl's sighs.

Mulan weaves while facing the door; her placement within the room indicates already her desire to leave. There is an important difference between Mulan and the girl in Sun Yunfeng's poem. Mulan is heard; the girl in Sun Yunfeng's poem hears and sees. Sun Yunfeng also quickly guides the reader into the mind of the girl so that the world is understood from her perspective. The bright moon is white as is the frost (reflecting the light of the moon), so that the moonlight already present in the room and in the mind of the girl brings the external world into the interior space. Outside already permeates inside. When the girl finally quits weaving and rolls up the screen, the poem not only launches into the cosmos, but also casts a glance back to another famous poem in the tradition, the fifth song of the 古詩十九 *Nineteen Ancient Songs* (c. 200 CE).

This poem recalls the story of 織女 Weaver Maid and 牛郎 Oxherd. There are many versions of this myth dating back thousands of years, but essentially their love is forbidden. They see each other from opposite sides of the Milky Way. The final two lines are echoed in Sun Yunfeng's poem (http://ctext.org/dictionary.pl?if=en&id=540575):

盈盈一水間，
脉脉不得語。

Lovely and tender, with the river between,
Longingly, they look but cannot gather the words.

In some versions of the myth they are allowed to meet once a year. When the Star River wears thin at the end of Sun Yunfeng's poem, it suggests that the moment for their reunion may be near. But just as Sun Yunfeng's travel poems always seem to end before any possible epiphany or moment of transcendence, this poem ends before the girl can witness this reunion, if it is possible at all. In the "Ballad of Mulan," Mulan will abandon her loom to take up arms (as in the Disney cartoon), but in Sun Yunfeng's poem the girl stops weaving because she is bored with it and would rather think about Chinese mythology and poetry. Unlike Sun Yunfeng, this girl is unable to gather the words. Although both the girl in the poem and Sun Yunfeng are denied experiences permitted men, the poet at least has the means and talent to express herself beyond inarticulate sighs.

When I asked earlier if Sun Yunfeng's "Ancient Feelings" were evidence of a woman pretending to be a man pretending to be a woman, perhaps I should have asked instead: is she a woman pretending to be a woman whose experience is wholly unlike her own? The first of these two poems represents a woman so strictly bounded by expectations that she looks only at her own face as she applies her eyebrows. She can see no further. In the second poem

24 *Sun Yunfeng*

the girl looks beyond herself, beyond her loom, beyond her room, beyond the courtyard and looks to the stars, which reflect back to her lines of a long-ago poem. The cruelty of Sun Yunfeng's travel poetry is that once the girl — or someone like her — can venture into the world beyond the empty courtyard, her experiences fall short of what she may have imagined them to be.

This chapter has been, in part, an argument that Sun Yunfeng deserves to be read well beyond the confines of Qing Women's Poetry. I would not dare ask David Damrosch to replace *Dream of the Red Chamber* with "Ancient Feelings," but certainly there is room for her and other poets like her somewhere along the axes of World Literature. The Tang poetry that is found in World Literature anthologies would become all the more impressive if its readers encountered later poetry (indeed, *much* later) so deeply indebted to it. And even a reading of *Dream of the Red Chamber*, despite my earlier insistence that it needs little contextualization to be appreciated, could only be enriched by learning something of the poetry contemporary to it, since the novel is full of poetry and evaluations of poetry, with the female characters no less engaged than the male. Despite the ever-expanding reach of World Literature, it nonetheless feels as if Sun Yunfeng has been relegated to a room deep within the palace of unread texts, waiting for a reader to notice her when stealing a glance across empty courtyards and around rolled-down pearl-encrusted screens.

Notes

1 Kenneth Rexroth included four of her poems in his *Women Poets of China* (1972) but it would be more than two decades before further poems of hers would be translated into English.

2 I've relied on J.D. Schmidt's *Harmony Garden. The Life, Literary Criticism, and Poetry of Yuan Mei (1716–1798)*, Kang-i Sun Chang and Haun Saussy's *Women Writers of Traditional China: An Anthology of Poetry and Criticism*, Susan Mann's "Learned Women in the Eighteenth Century," and Liuxi Meng's *Poetry as Power. Yuan Mei's Female Disciple Qu Bingyun (1767–1810)* for the details of Sun Yunfeng's biography. Most of the details are extracted not only from Yuan Mei's voluminous writings, but also from entries in nineteenth- and early twentieth-century biographical dictionaries.

3 All Tang poetry is taken from the online version of the Beijing 1960 *Quan Tangshi* (Complete Tang Poetry), which was originally edited by 彭定求 Peng Dingqiu in the late seventeenth century.

4 The text is taken from an electronic version of the twelfth-century *Yuefu Shiji* (Collection of Music Bureau Poems) at http://ctext.org/library.pl?if=en&res=77652.

2 Paul Claudel (1868–1955)
Lost before Translation

I am not going to make a case, even tongue-in-cheek, for the inclusion of Paul Claudel in any anthology of World Literature. Paul Claudel is not to everyone's taste, and certainly not to mine. Nonetheless, if practicing World Literature means learning the history of trying to understand literatures and cultures distant from one's own, then it makes sense to pause on the speed bump called Claudel on that never-ending, ever-lengthening path to intercultural comprehension. When I tried to find out when, where, how and why this poet may have been anthologized in English in recent years, much to my surprise I found him not in any anthology of World Literature, but instead in an anthology of Modern *Japanese* Literature. These thirty lines translated by Miriam Silverberg from a 1927 poem by the Marxist Japanese poet Nakano Shigeharu make me want to start studying Japanese right away. This poem is so delightful and profound that once I master Japanese (in my next lifetime, if it is full of lengthy sabbaticals) and read all Nakano's poetry, I will then clamor to have him admitted into the pantheon of World Literature, regardless of where he has slid along the World Lit axes. Unfortunately, I would then have to find some way to make a case for Claudel, otherwise the World Literature reader would be puzzled by this poem, which strikes me as the best brief summary I have ever read (*pace* Wikipédia) of what Paul Claudel means:

Paul Claudel was a poet
Paul Claudel was an ambassador
And France occupied the Ruhr

Romain Rolland fled to Jesus
Vladimir Ilyich returned to Russia
And Paul Claudel wrote poetry

26 *Paul Claudel*

Japan sent troops to Siberia
Fatty Semenov came running
And Paul Claudel wrote poetry

The farmers of France saved their money
The rich took that away
And the rich prayed to Mary

And Paul Claudel prayed to Mary
And Paul Claudel became the French Ambassador to Japan
And Paul Claudel wrote poetry

Paul Claudel wrote poetry
Paul Claudel circled the moat
Paul Claudel played the shamisen
Paul Claudel danced kabuki
Paul Claudel did foreign relations

Ahh and then
Finally one day
Paul Claudel
Memorialized Charles-Louis Philippe
the ambassador on Philippe!

Ahh the great Paul Claudel
Paul Claudel ambassador they say is a poet
"Our little Philippe" will
From within his humble grave most likely say
"Paul Claudel became ambassador?" (Nagano, 606)[1]

This wicked poem works through a series of apparent non-sequiturs. World-shaking events such as France's occupation of the Ruhr when Germany fell behind in its reparation payments in 1923, Lenin's return to Russia from exile, and Japanese intervention in the Russian Civil War following the Russian Revolution ("Fatty Semenov") are juxtaposed with the line "Paul Claudel wrote poetry," an event less world-rattling. Once the poem has deflated the importance of his writing poetry, it puts his prayers to Mary and his ambassadorship to Japan on the same level. I am not entirely sure what to make of the reference to Romain Rolland, who was a towering, Nobel-Prize-winning figure in French Literature when this poem was composed, but describing him as "fled to Jesus" can hardly

Paul Claudel 27

be considered a sign of admiration. Rolland's star has long since faded, so that he has certainly disappeared along one or both of the axes of World Literature without much chance of rolling back, despite his World Literature-affirming Nobel Prize (Claudel never got one, nor did Nakano for that matter). The noveliest-died-young Charles-Louis Philippe who débuts near the end of the poem, for his part has all but disappeared from memory, whether in France or elsewhere. It is not to Paul Claudel's credit that Nakano imagines Philippe wondering, not even from beyond the grave but from within it, at Claudel's elevation to ambassador to Japan.

Perhaps the funniest part of the poem — and most relevant to my purpose — has Claudel circling the moat (apparently of the Imperial Palace in Tokyo, which he was wont to do [Kawakami, 120]), playing the shamisen, a traditional Japanese string instrument, and, more hilarious yet, dancing the Kabuki — which is not exactly something anyone, let alone a poetry-writing, foreign-relations-doing, Charles-Louis Philippe-lamenting Frenchman, can simply leap to his feet and start doing. It also incorrectly associates Claudel with Kabuki when, in fact, he was influenced instead by another Japanese theatrical tradition, Nôh (Micciolo, note 20, 328; Gillespie, 58). My best guess is that Nakano is mocking, along with Claudel, the Western tendency to conflate Nôh with the better-known Kabuki. As for the shamisen, in 1926 Claudel published a dialog between a "Poëte" and a "shamisen" in *Commerce*, a magazine among whose editors was no less a figure than Paul Valéry (Claudel, 1970, 111). In it the shamisen seems reluctant to have its strings plucked by the Frenchman. No one can doubt that Nakano was well informed about the details and fruits of Claudel's interest in Japanese culture. Perhaps this poem marks a secondary path by which Claudel enters World Literature, one that bypasses English, at least until it appears in the *Columbia Anthology of Modern Japanese Literature*. Maybe World Literature should be called Worlds Literature instead.

In fairness to Paul Claudel, he was once famous enough in the English-speaking world to appear on the March 11, 1927 cover of *Time*, captioned "The Ambassador." In recent years he has experienced something of a World Literature renaissance. To Nahano's poem in the *Columbia Anthology of Modern Japanese Literature* one might add two of his own poems in Mary Ann Caws's 2004 *Yale Anthology of Modern French Poetry*, and one poem in a 2012 reprint of Dover's 1969 *Invitation to French Poetry*. In 2004 his *Connaissance de l'Est* appeared in a new English translation by James Lawler as *Knowing the East*, so it may be the case that Claudel has

28 *Paul Claudel*

retreated from the edge of the Not-World-Enough-Literature abyss, regardless of any ambivalence I might feel about him.

Whether or not Claudel is considered a denizen of World Literature (and if he is, please do not make me teach, or even re-read, his many tiresome plays), his account of how he comes to know the East may serve as a cautionary tale for World Lit's practitioners. I have in mind the now (in)famous early 1990s exchange between Steven Owen and Rey Chow, its fall-out and more than two decades of after-life. Owen, perhaps the greatest Sinologist of his generation, wrote a review for *World Poetry* about a new translation of several of 北岛 Bei Dao's (1949–) poems. He uses the review to excoriate a certain kind of apparently ready-for-translation contemporary Chinese poetry, or as he would have it, a world poetry masquerading as Chinese poetry. Three years later, Chow, so lionized she has her own *Rey Chow Reader*, opens her book *Writing Diaspora: Tactics of Intervention in Contemporary Cultural Studies*, by berating Owen for projecting onto Bei Dao's poetry his own anxiety about the devaluation of his field (Classical Chinese Poetry), which is threatened by the rise of a modern Chinese poetry that she believes owes nothing to it. To illuminate this debate, if it can be called such, I will first look closely at "Religion du signe" (Religion of the sign), a brief narrative by Claudel that first appeared in *La Revue blanche* in 1897 (Bush, 40). Three years later it would be published as part of the first edition of *Knowing the East*. In 1925 it is published yet again as part of *Philosophie du livre*.

There can be little doubt that Claudel considered "Religion of the sign" a key part of his oeuvre. It begins (complete text to be found in Claudel, 1920, 48–52):

> Que d'autres découvrent dans la rangée des caractères chinois, ou une tête de mouton, ou des mains, les jambes d'un homme, le soleil qui se lève derrière un arbre. J'y poursuis pour ma part un lacs plus inextricable.

> Let others find in the vast range of Chinese characters a sheep's head, a pair of hands, a man's legs, or the sun rising behind a tree. I myself am in search of a snare from which there is no escape.

The Chinese characters he gives as examples seem to be taken from a reference work compiled by Léon Wieger (1856–1933), a Jesuit missionary whose translations from Classical Chinese into French were as seminal for the field of Sinology in France as those by James

Legge (1815–1897), also a missionary, into English were in Britain (Hellerstein, 286). Despite his reliance on Wieger, Claudel nonetheless rejects his way of reading Chinese characters. In 1925, when Claudel looks back at his twenty years in the East during a lecture titled *Une Promenade à travers la littérature japonaise* (A stroll through Japanese Literature) he contrasts his method of learning about China and Japan with those of scholars. Since this lecture coincided with the republication of "Religion of the Sign," it is not unreasonable to imagine that Claudel had not fully forgotten this earlier text when he said

> Je ne suis pas, malgré mes quinze ans de Chine et mes cinq ans de Japon, ce que les Anglais appellent un *scholar*, un spécialiste de l'Extrême-Orient, dont j'ignore les différents idiomes. Je n'ai poursuivi aucune étude méthodique et toute ma connaissance du pays résulte de l'atmosphère dont je me suis laissé imprégner, des circonstances, des entretiens, des excursions, des impressions recueillies au fil des jours et des nuits et des lectures plus ou moins incohérentes que j'ai picorées de tous côtés. En résumé je ne suis qu'un amateur, qu'un curieux…. (cited in Mayau, 156)

> I am not, despite my fifteen years in China and my five in Japan, what the English call a *scholar*, a specialist of the Far East, whose various idioms I do not know. I have never studied it in any methodical way and everything I know about this part of the world is the result of letting its atmosphere permeate me, of circumstances, conversations, excursions, impressions gathered night and day, and readings that I pecked at randomly here and there. In other words, I'm just a curious amateur….

His lapse into English here is puzzling. Is a scholar so different from an *érudit* or a *savant*, two words that could translate *scholar*? Etymologically, a scholar has been schooled, a *savant* knows and an *érudit* has been instructed. Claiming to be neither schooled nor instructed, Claudel also insists that he does not know the way a *savant* knows, since he has come to know the East not in the sense of *savoir* (to know facts) but in the sense of *connaître* (to know through experience) as the title *Connaissance de l'est* suggests.

Returning to "Religion of the Sign," although Claudel relied heavily on Wieger for his knowledge of Chinese characters, he nonetheless rejects his way of knowing (mere *savoir*) and offers his own theory of how Chinese characters work, without explaining how he has arrived

30   *Paul Claudel*

at it. He begins with the sort of sweeping ahistorical statement that I caution my undergraduates to avoid in their term papers:

> Toute écriture commence par le trait ou ligne, qui, un dans sa continuité, est le signe pur de l'individu. Ou donc la ligne est horizontale, comme toute chose qui dans le seul parallélisme à son principe trouve une raison d'être suffisante; ou, verticale comme l'arbre et l'homme, elle indique l'acte et pose l'affirmation; ou, oblique, elle marque le mouvement et le *sens*.

> All writing begins with a trace or line, which, integral in its continuity, is the pure sign for what cannot be divided. So the line is either horizontal, like all things that only in parallelism find reason to be adequate to its principle; or it is vertical like a tree or a man, indicating an action or assertion; or it is oblique, marking movement and *meaning*.

That's a long way from a *tête de mouton*. Claudel is certainly correct to disavow any pretention to scholarship. This passage seems to relate Claudel's own unsubstantiated mythology of writing's origin.

Having replaced Wieger's figural theory of Chinese characters with his abstract reading of all writing, Claudel prepares to make the essential gesture of drawing a line between West and East.

> La lettre romaine a eu pour principe la ligne verticale; le caractère chinois paraît avoir l'horizontale comme trait essentiel. La lettre d'un impérieux jambage affirme que la chose est telle; le caractère *est* la chose tout entière qu'il signifie.

> The Latin letter was based on the vertical line; the essential line of the Chinese character seems to be horizontal. A letter composed of an imperious downstroke affirms that the thing is so; the character *is* the thing it signifies in its entirety.

Wieger's mutton-heads and suns setting behind trees might be off the mark, but Claudel replaces them with a fundamental misunderstanding of how the Chinese character functions, one that he shared with Ezra Pound and that persists until this day. It is impossible for an element of a writing system *to be* the thing it signifies, even in strange and far-off China. A reader can page through Wieger's long book about Chinese characters and understand how he might see a resemblance between 東, especially the archaic version he provides next to the modern character, and a rising sun with a tree in the way

(Wieger, 341). He relied on traditional Chinese etymologies, which were not necessarily accurate, but at least had the benefit of being indigenous. However, if one reads Chinese (a big if), one can stare at a Chinese character for years and fail to make any sense out of Claudel's gibberish. Though to be fair, what Claudel says about the Latin alphabet is equally silly. Despite centuries of claims to the contrary, the Chinese writing system, while not an alphabet, nonetheless is in large part a phonetic system. It does not function the way Euro-American readers expect a phonetic system to function, since they have been conditioned to understand that only alphabets can be phonetic. It is not difficult, however, to demonstrate that Chinese characters are also phonetic. Even someone who cannot read Chinese might notice that 馬 *mǎ* (horse), 罵 *mà* (curse), 媽 *mā* (mother), 瑪 *mǎ* (agate), 螞 *mā* (ant) and 嗎 *ma* (indicates a question) share two things in common: 馬 and *ma*. The character 馬 when used as a component of another, more complex, character is not semantic; it is phonetic and indicates *ma*. The other component of these characters indicates the class into which each belongs. The 女 in 媽 indicates that it is a female something that sounds like *mā*. The 玉 before 瑪 indicates that it is a gemstone that sounds like *mǎ* and so on. If you cannot read Chinese, you could contemplate 馬 at length and never recognize it as the word for horse, because it is *not* a horse, it *signifies* horse. A Chinese reader does not look at 媽 and think of a horse, but instead thinks of the word for mother. A Chinese character does not be, it signifies; it is not the thing itself, it is referential. Even the image of something, which a Chinese character even as Claudel misunderstands it is far from being, is not the thing itself, but referential.

Nonetheless, Claudel continues in the same vein:

> L'une et l'autre sont également des signes; qu'on prenne, par exemple, les chiffres, l'une et l'autre en sont également les images abstraites. Mais la lettre est par essence analytique: tout mot qu'elle constitue est une énonciation successive d'affirmations que l'oeil et la voix épellent; à l'unité elle ajoute sur une même ligne l'unité, et le vocable précaire dans une continuelle variation se fait et se modifie. Le signe chinois développe, pour ainsi dire, le chiffre; et, l'appliquant à la série des êtres, il en différencie indéfiniment le *caractère*. Le mot existe par la succession des lettres, le caractère par la proportion des traits. Et ne peut-on rêver que dans celui-ci la ligne horizontale indique, par exemple, l'espèce, la verticale, l'individu, les obliques dans

32 *Paul Claudel*

leurs mouvements divers l'ensemble des propriétés et des énergies qui donnent au tout son *sens*, le point, suspendu dans le blanc, quelque rapport qu'il ne convient que de sous-entendre? On peut donc voir dans le caractère chinois un être schématique, une personne scripturale, ayant, comme un être qui vit, sa nature et ses modalités, son action propre et sa vertu intime, sa structure et sa physionomie.

Par là s'explique cette piété des Chinois à l'écriture; on incinère avec respect le plus humble papier que marque le mystérieux vestige. Le signe est un être, et, de ce fait qu'il est général, il devient sacré. La représentation de l'idée en est ici, en quelque sorte, l'idole. Telle est la base de cette religion scripturale qui est particulière à la Chine. Hier j'ai visité un temple Confucianiste.

Each one of these, letter and character, is to the same degree a sign; let's take numerals as an example; in each case it is an abstract image. The letter, however, essentially requires analysis: every word it forms is a series of enunciated statements that the eye and the voice spell out; to a unit on the same line is added another unit, and the precarious vocable through a continual process of variation both takes form and is transformed. The Chinese sign develops, so to speak, the numerical figure; and, applying it to a series of beings, produces an endless variation of *characters*. A word exists thanks to a succession of letters, the character thanks to the proportion of its lines. Is it impossible to imagine that in this way a horizontal lign indicates, for example, a species, while the vertical line indicates an individual, and the oblique lines in their various movements indicate the totality of properties and energies that give everything *meaning*, while the period, suspended on the white page indicates some relationship that can only be surmised? As for the Chinese character, there is nothing to see but a schematic being, a written person, having, like any living being, its own nature and modalities, its own action and intimate quality, its own structure and its own physiognomy.

This would explain why the Chinese have a pious regard for the written; they respectfully burn the most humble scrap of paper marked with these mysterious traces. The sign is a being, and, in this way generalized, becomes sacred as well. The representation of an idea here is then, in some way, an idol. Such is the foundation of the religion of the written specific to China. Yesterday I visited a Confucian temple.

Having spelled out in great detail how a word constructed out of letters differs from a Chinese character, Claudel suddenly departs the world inside his head, where words in the Western sense (it is important to understand, however, that Chinese characters also form words) are powerful through their adherence to generalizable characteristics, while Chinese characters suffer the weakness of the mere individual. Claudel's phrase "Yesterday I visited a Confucian temple" seems to come from nowhere. Claudel offers no prelude, no liaison to a previous sentence, no context, no preparation. This is true both in the recounted historical moment — where *is* this temple, *how* did he get there, and *why* is he going? — and in its recounting, for neither does the reader know how s/he has suddenly arrived at this moment in the text itself. One minute Claudel speaks from a world of abstraction and generalization and then all of a sudden he has been to a real Confucian temple. One minute the reader is puzzling through Claudel's flights of fancy and then all of a sudden s/he has tagged along to an as-yet-undescribed Confucian temple.

How Claudel has arrived at this unnamed, unlocated, unspecified Confucian temple (he is attached to a French consulate, he is a poet, he will some far-off day dance the kabuki and pluck at the strings of a reluctant samisen) is left unwritten, for the vast machinery of imperial France that has conspired to enable the journey that replaces *savoir* with *connaissance* and thereby allows intimate knowledge to supersede scholarship, however faulty, need not be written into the tale to which he will return nearly thirty years later as emblematic of his knowing the East. Claudel wastes no time in immersing the reader in the details of this visit.

Il se trouve dans un quartier solitaire où tout sent la désertion de la chute. Dans le silence et les solennelles ardeurs du soleil de trois heures, nous suivons la rue sinueuse. Notre entrée ne sera point par la grande porte dont les vantaux ont pourri dans leur fermeture: que la haute stèle marquée de l'officielle inscription bilingue garde le seuil âgé! Une femme courte, râblée comme un cochon, nous ouvre des passages latéraux et d'un pied qui sonne nous pénétrons dans l'enclos désert.

It's found in a solitary neighborhood where everything reeks of the emptiness following the end of the world. In the silence and blazing heat of three PM we make our way down the snaking street. We will by no means enter through the great gate whose doors have rotted since they were last closed: may the

34 *Paul Claudel*

lofty stelae marked with an official bilingual inscription guard the ancient threshold! A short woman, broad-backed like a pig, opens the side passages for us and we penetrate the deserted enclosure with noisy steps.

Claudel goes from "I" to "we" without explanation. Is he joined by a companion? A minder? A guide? A retinue? An entourage? What Claudel elides is the support network his coming to know the East requires; he can pretend that this knowledge is randomly generated, all about atmosphere and impressions, but even the pig-like woman is prerequisite to his penetration of the abandoned temple. It is unfortunate that the only other human being specifically mentioned in the piece is described as being like a pig, but I suppose her sub-humanity only further increases the faux sense of solitude and individual discovery that Claudel wants to convey.

The adventure continues. The pig-woman might be the one with the power to open side passages, but Claudel has an arsenal of classical architectural vocabulary with which he can signal his appreciation of the temple.

Par les proportions de sa cour et des péristyles qui l'encadrent, par les larges entrecolonnements et les lignes horizontales de sa façade, par la répétition de ses deux énormous toits, qui d'un mouvement un relèvent ensemble leur noire et puissante volute, par la disposition symétrique des deux petits pavillons qui le précedent et qui au sévère ensemble ajoutent l'agrément grotesque de leurs chapeaux octogones, l'édifice, appliquant les seuls lois essentielles de l'architecture, a l'aspect savant de l'évidence, la beauté, pour tout dire, classique, due à une observation exquise de la règle.

Le temple se compose de deux parties. Je suppose que les allées hypœthrales avec la rangée des tablettes, chacune précédée de l'étroit et long autel de pierre, qui en occupent la paroi, offrent à une révérence rapide la série extérieure des préceptes. Mais levant le pied pour franchir le seuil barré au pas, nous pénétrons dans l'ombre du sanctuaire.

By the proportions of its courtyard and the peristyles that frame it, by the intercolumniation and the horizontal lines of its façade, by the repetition of its two enormous roofs, that in a single movement lift together their dark and powerful volute, by the symmetrical placement of two little pavilions in front of it, adding to the severity of the architectural complex the grotesque charm of their octagonal hats, the edifice, applying just the essential laws of architecture, achieves self-evident mastery of classical beauty through an exquisite adherence to its rules.

The temple can be divided into two sections. I guess that the hypethral alleyways with their array of tablets occupying the walls, each preceded by a long, narrow stone altar, offer an external series of precepts for the worshiper pressed for time. But lifting our feet to cross the threshold forbidden to step on, we penetrate into the darkness of the sanctuary.

Although Claudel has tried to distinguish the Latin alphabet from Chinese characters, the language he uses to describe this Confucian temple is borrowed entirely from the vocabulary of classical architecture. There is no attempt to initiate the reader into the language of Chinese architecture. Words like "péristyle," "entrecolonnement" and "hypethral" are not common in everyday French and may even serve to prevent the reader from visualizing the buildings at all.

Claudel turns from this highly specialized language of classical architecture once he begins to describe the sanctuary. It is finally at this point that the reader might begin to understand the relationship between Claudel's description of Chinese characters and his visit to the Confucian temple, which up to this point has seemed like a non-sequitur.

La salle vaste et haute a l'air, comme du fait d'une présence occulte, plus vide, et le silence, avec le voile de l'obscurité, l'occupe. Point d'ornéments, point de statues. De chaque côté de la halle, nous distinguons, entre leurs rideaux, de grandes inscriptions, et, au devant, des autels. Mais au milieu du temple, précédés de cinq monumentales pièces de pierre, trois vases et deux chandeliers, sous un édifice d'or, baldaquin ou tabernacle, qui l'encadre de ses ouvertures successives, sur une stèle verticale sont inscrits quatre caractères.

The vast and soaring room seems yet more empty, as if due to an occult presence, and silence, veiled by darkness, fills it. No decoration or statues at all. On each side of the hall, we distinguish, between their curtains, some huge inscriptions, and, before them, altars. But in the middle of the temple, behind five monumental works of stone, three vases and two chandeliers, beneath a gold edifice, which is either a baldaquin or tabernacle, that frames it within a series of openings, is a vertical stelae on which are inscibed four characters.

36   *Paul Claudel*

It now seems clear that the point of this journey is to lead the reader from beyond the temple complex, through winding streets, around gates that can no longer be opened, down a series of side passages guided by a pig-woman, across a courtyard, over a threshold, into a dark sanctuary, and, finally under a gold baldaquin to see four Chinese characters inscribed on a stone monument. Might a reader dare wish that *these* four characters are the very characters that have led Claudel to his own theorization of the Chinese writing system, since rather than merely read about them, he has seen them with his own eyes?

And, indeed, Claudel begins to describe the writing on the stelae.

> L'écriture a ceci de mystérieux qu'elle parle. Nul moment n'en marque la durée, ici nulle position, le commencement du signe sans âge: il n'est bouche qui le profère. Il existe, et l'assistant face à face considère le nom lisible.
>
> Enonciation avec profondeur dans le reculement des ors assombris du baldaquin, le signe entre les deux colonnes que revêt l'enroulement mystique du dragon, signifie son propre silence. L'immense salle rouge imite la couleur de l'obscurité, et ses piliers sont revêtus d'une laque écarlate. Seuls, au milieu du temple, devant le sacré mot, deux fûts de granit blanc semblent des témoins, et la nudité même, religieuse et abstraite, du lieu.

> Writing has something of the mysterious that it speaks. No moment marks its duration, no position marks the ageless sign's beginning: there is no mouth to proffer it. It exists, and the attendant facing it considers the legible name.
>
> A resonant enunciation in the distant spaces of the shadowed gold of the baldaquin, the sign between columns garbed in the mystical coils of the dragon signifies its own silence. The immense red room imitates the color of darkness, and its pillars are arrayed in scarlet lacquer. Alone, in the middle of the temple, before the sacred word, two shafts of white granite seem to be witnesses, and at the same time the very nakedness, religious and abstract, of the place.

Claudel leads the reader — leads his party, his retinue, maybe even the pig-woman — to the darkness at the center of the sanctuary of this temple that seems to represent the Middle Kingdom itself. And at this darkness in the center of a Chinese temple he finds the source of the very mystery of writing itself: he can't read it.

Yes, writing has something mysterious about it; especially if you do not or cannot read it. Claudel does not seem to have been a practical joker or to have been blessed with a great sense of humor; at least none of his contemporaries seem to have remarked on it. So I will assume that the mysticality of the unread Chinese characters is meant to be taken seriously. Claudel does consider the possibility of someone facing the word and finding it legible. The French word "assistant" is general enough (here does it mean "someone who is present at something"?) that I cannot be sure if he intends a worshipper or perhaps someone responsible for the upkeep of the sanctuary. Considering the general illiteracy of women outside the ruling class in late nineteenth-century China, this person is unlikely to be the pig-woman (pigs can't read, after all). Whoever it might be facing the "sign" must be absent at the moment Claudel and his band penetrate the sanctuary, because he does not whisper in Claudel's ear the meaning of the four characters. The written Chinese language, the ostensible goal of this journey, gives way to the shadowed gold overhead, the darkening red of the walls and the columns, and the two white shafts of granite. Having reached the four characters, Claudel turns from them to contemplate the play of color in the sanctuary and thereby makes them disappear into the abstraction with which he began "Religion of the Sign."

Claudel's knowledge of the East and *Knowing the East* depends, oddly enough, on not knowing it. While Edward Said's *Orientalism* famously argues that the West fabricates the Orient by constructing a knowledge of it that undergirds the power of Europeans and North Americans over the Middle East, Claudel's point — even if it is not one he intended to make — is that knowledge (*savoir*) is irrelevant. Claudel can remain willfully ignorant — refuse to see and refuse to read — and still his posse, including the helpful pig-woman, will accompany him, guide him, enable him to gather *connaissance* out of nothing other than the power to compel others to do his will as the representative of a European imperial power at its height. Simply being proximate, close, intimate, penetrating all the way to the dark red center, is enough to convince Claudel that he knows something that some French — well, Alsatian, to be precise — Jesuit gone native poring over Chinese tomes cannot. It was not the *savants, érudits* or scholars who ran roughshod over the East, whether Near or Far, but the mere amateurs.

If I had written this chapter in imitation of Claudel, I would have chosen to forego all mention of Steven Owen, Rey Chow and Bei Dao until this sentence, and then would have written "And

38 *Paul Claudel*

yesterday I read a book review," or better yet, "Yesterday I read the introduction to a book that wrote about the beginning of another book that wrote about a book review." On November 19, 1990 *The New Republic* published Steven Owen's review of Bonnie McDougall's translation of Bei Dao's *The August Sleepwalker*. Not much of the article entitled "What Is World Poetry?" is devoted to the book under review itself. Instead Owen decries the rise of "World Poetry," unmoored from this or that national literature, because it encourages poets to write what is easily translated into other languages, most often English. What is spectacularly odd about the article is that Owen constructs an abstract, imaginary "World Poetry" that he describes but never peoples with actual poets. When he finally gets around to mentioning a real poet — Bei Dao, happily, since the book ostensibly under consideration is his — he all but excuses him from the accusation of World Poetry:

> ...it is to Bei Dao's credit (and to Bonnie McDougall's) that *The August Sleepwalker* is freer of large doses of Nutrasweet than virtually any other modern Chinese poetry I have read. Bei Dao's talents, and McDougall's considerable skill as a translator, make these among the only translations of modern Chinese poetry that are not, by and large, embarrassing. (30)

The praise is tepid and follows a series of quotations from Bei Dao's poetry that Owen likens to his own scribblings at age 14, which he claims to have wisely destroyed. He praises the translator and yet also says

> We must wonder if such collections of poetry in translation become publishable only because the publisher and the readership have been assured that the poetry was lost in translation. But what if the poetry wasn't lost in translation? What if this is it? (31)

He then answers his own question with: "This *is* it." However, he makes not one reference to any of the Chinese originals, never points to any divergence from the Chinese text in the English translation, or, conversely, to demonstrate that there is a perfect correspondence between the Chinese and the English. Apparently, McDougall's great achievement was to translate bad Chinese poetry into equally bad English poetry. If this is the case, certainly Owen could have provided an example or two. To simply assert that nothing is lost in translation without evidence is, at best, unscholarly. *The New Republic* presumably asked Owen to review the book because he is a scholar of poetry, although perhaps a specialist in poetry of a millennium ago was not the most obvious choice to review a volume of contemporary Chinese poetry.

His pronouncements about how today's Chinese feel about contemporary poetry are also weirdly unsourced. When Owen writes about his Chinese friend who writes verse in both "classical Chinese" and in "vernacular Chinese" in order to categorize one as more Chinese than the other, one wants to ask, Well WHO IS IT? as well as, what does that even mean? (28). He turns from this unnamed authority to "Chinese readers of 'New Poetry' with whom I have spoken" in order to compare Bei Dao's most recent poetry with his politically engaged poetry of the past (31). Although he does not consider them sub-human, the function of this poetry-writing Chinese friend and these Chinese aficionados of Chinese poetry he spoke to is not unlike that of Claudel's pig-woman opening doors to passages to which he would otherwise not have access. Unlike Claudel, who cannot read the Chinese characters, Owen seems to choose not to and simply assumes that nothing is lost in translation. Since Owen can't be bothered to look, Bei Dao's Chinese text is lost *before* rather than *in* translation.

Rey Chow's reaction is harsh, but not swift, since it appears three years later.

> For Owen, the inferior poetic skills of Bei Dao are, ostensibly, what he considers to be signs of the "third world poet's" inability to rise to the grandeur of his own cultural past. But this moralistic indictment of the other's infidelity masks a more fundamental anxiety. This is the anxiety that the Chinese past which he has undertaken to penetrate is evaporating and that the sinologist himself is the abandoned subject. What this means, significantly, is that a situation has been constructed in which the historical relation between the "first world" and the "third world" is reversed: writers of the "third world" like Bei Dao now appear not as the oppressed but as oppressors, who aggress against the "first world" sinologist by robbing him of his love. Concluding his essay sourly with the statement, "Welcome to the late twentieth century," Owen's real complaint is that *he* is the victim of a monstrous world order in front of which a sulking impotence like his is the only claim to truth. (Chow, 4)

40   *Paul Claudel*

Chow's use of sexually charged language cannot be unintentional: fidelity, penetrate, love, impotence. The attack is personal but scattershot. Is Owen acting like a jealous lover who has had his love stolen away, is he a moralizing nag whining about someone else's infidelity, or is he simply unable to get it up? Metaphorically and academically, of course.

As Damrosch points out in his charitable analysis of Chow,

> The problem for a nonspecialist reader — apart from the danger of the critical prose bursting into flames in your hands — is that Chow is so deeply committed to her position that she doesn't see any need to combat Owen's views by discussing a single line of Bei Dao's poetry. (20)

Is it that Chow doesn't see any need to discuss a single line of Bei Dao or that she can't be bothered? She not only doesn't discuss a single line of Bei Dao's poetry, but also doesn't even mention one. Not only does the question of whether Bei Dao's poetry is any good not interest her, his poetry doesn't interest her either. Chow's personal attack on Owen (he's not only impotent but anxious about it, too) does, however, remind the reader that Owen's review of Bei Dao's poetry is personal. It is not based on *savoir*, although Owen is truly a scholar, *érudit* and *savant*, but on *connaissance*. His knowledge of what's wrong with Bei Dao's poetry is based on proximity and intimacy: he has a friend who writes Chinese poetry and talks to Chinese people who are interested in poetry, therefore Owen just knows, like Claudel, without having to bother with reading the Chinese. Apparently, Chow need not even bother to read the English translation.

To his credit, Damrosch tries to remedy this lacuna by comparing two different translations of a poem by Bei Dao. Not surprisingly, they are quite different, but in his analysis Damrosch overreaches. He performs close readings of both versions without any reference to the Chinese and in so doing reveals the fundamental weakness of World Literature: there is no text. As far as I can tell, neither Owen nor Chow read Bei Dao in Chinese; one of Owen's friends did (or at least read some modern Chinese poetry, whether or not by Bei Dao) and that's good enough for him, while I suspect that Chow doesn't much care for poetry anyway (references to poetry beyond bashing Owen in *The Rey Chow Reader* turn out to be really about theorists such as Benjamin and Hegel; poetry is fodder for "Theory," which seems to me as disrespectful of poetry as complaining that someone's poetry isn't classical enough). As much as I admire the brilliance of Damrosch's readings of works far beyond the stretch of his linguistic abilities (I feel confident in asserting that he does not read cuneiform or speak Babylonian, for instance, but he nonetheless writes thrillingly and persuasively about *Gilgamesh*), I am not convinced that he can look at a translation of a modern Chinese poem, compare it to another translation, and then point out "an underlying word play in the original," especially since there is no hint of such word play in the other translation (23). Literary criticism is not magic, not even World Literature literary criticism.

Since the poem in question, "The Answer," is Bei Dao's most famous, it was not at all difficult to find, although it may have been less readily accessible in 1990, 1993 or 2003. It pops up in 百度 *Baidu*, roughly the Chinese equivalent of Wikipedia (http://baike.baidu.com/item/回答/5948321). I give the first two couplets in Chinese characters, followed by a transliteration so that the non-Chinese reader can get a sense of how the poem sounds.

回答
卑鄙是卑鄙者的通行证，
高尚是高尚者的墓志铭。
看吧，在那镀金的天空中，
飘满了死者弯曲的倒影。

huí dá
bēibǐ shì bēibǐzhěde tōngxíngzhèng,
gāoshàng shì gāoshàngzhěde mùzhìmíng.
kànba zài nà dùjīnde tiānkōngzhōng,
piāopiāole sǐzhě wānqūde daòyǐng.

Translating the first couplet as directly as possible results in

Baseness is the one-who-practices-baseness's pass,
Nobility is the one-who-practices-nobility's epitaph.

What's lost in translation, *pace* Owen, is the use of a common construction of classical Chinese using 者, which means here something like, "one who is" or "one who does." The other very Chinese element of this couplet — beyond the fact that using the couplet as the building block of a poem is itself a carryover from classical Chinese poetry — is the parallelism between the first and second lines. All the grammatical elements line up in the same order, which all but demands that the reader compare each element in order to determine its meaning.

42   *Paul Claudel*

Damrosch cites two translations, the first by McDougall and the second by Donald Finkel (cited in Damrosch, 23).[2]

> Debasement is the password of the base.
> Nobility the epitaph of the noble.
>
> The scoundrel carries his baseness around like an ID card.
> The honest man bears his honor like an epitaph.

It isn't so much word play that's in question here, but repetition: baseness and baseness + 者. Bei Dao uses this construction to turn a characteristic into a person who embodies it. To my eyes it is mere tautology, lazy and obvious. It's bad poetry not because it ignores the heritage of Classical Chinese Poetry (in fact, it doesn't ignore it at all), but because it is flat and boring. Honestly, the lines read better in English than they do in Chinese. Something has indeed been lost in translation: tedium. McDougall's version is closer to the original, which may account for why Damrosch finds it inferior to Finkel's version; the original is also inferior to Finkel's version. Please, Rey Chow, failing to admire this couplet does not demonstrate my impotence.

The second couplet is at least imagistic. Again, the first translation is by McDougall and the second by Finkel.

> See how the gilded sky is covered
> With the drifting twisted shadows of the dead.
>
> Look — the gilded sky is swimming
> with undulant reflections of the dead.

I am somewhat puzzled that both McDougall and Finkel feel compelled to add a verb at the end of the first line, since there is no verb in the Chinese, but I suppose that it is difficult otherwise to construct a comprehensible line of English verse. Here is my feeble attempt to adhere as closely to the Chinese:

> Look! Up there in that gold-plated sky:
> the floating-packed-together dead's warped inverted images.

I don't know what this means, but the complex image does capture one's attention. I do not pretend to be scholar, *savant* or *érudit* when it comes to Modern Chinese Poetry. I read a great deal of it in the late 1980s and early 1990s, but after the marvelous poet 顧城 Gu

Cheng (1956–1993), who had been very kind and generous in sharing his poetry with me, committed suicide immediately after murdering his wife, I stopped reading contemporary Chinese poetry for ten years. My proximity to Gu Cheng during our all-too-brief correspondence does not lead me to claim *connaissance* of Modern Chinese Poetry either, but these four lines of poetry from Bei Dao are not particularly challenging or, frankly, interesting, which was at least part of Owen's point.

The penultimate line of the poem includes a reference to "pictographs" (McDougall) or "that ancient ideogram," either of which sets off alarm bells, considering the long, unhappy history of Euro-American misunderstanding of the nature of the Chinese character. The Chinese is 象形文字. A 象形 can either refer to a pictogram in general, or within the context of Classical Chinese, refers to one of the six traditional categories of Chinese characters, those believed to have originated as stylized representations of what it intended to represent (such as 馬 above). 文字 refers to written language or script. If Bei Dao had intended to be specifically Chinese in his reference, he would have left off 文字 or replaced it with 漢字, which is the modern Chinese word for "Chinese character." In other words, Bei Dao has chosen a Chinese word that may refer not only to Chinese characters, but to Egyptian hieroglyphs as well. This word is not an attempt to sprinkle some local color onto some World Poetry.

Since Bei Dao here at the end of the poem has redirected the attention of the reader back to the sky to look at a constellation, I would hazard to guess that he is striving for the universal rather than the particular (which would also explain why the view of the sky is now unobstructed by images of dead bodies, as it was at the beginning). Damrosch appreciates the Finkel translation for "using Ezra Pound's term of choice for Chinese characters," because it assorts "well with the debt to American modernism that Owen and others have identified in Bei Dao's work" (Damrosch, 23). Unfortunately, here Finkel's translation is not only wrong, but also seriously misleading, since a different Chinese word 指事, another of the six traditional categories of Chinese characters, would be better translated as ideogram, which is not the same as a pictogram. Bei Dao isn't looking to Ezra Pound and his grotesque misunderstanding of the Chinese character, but to the heavens; constellations as patterns imposed by human beings on the chaos of the skies are evidence of a connection to the distant past and the future. The path to freedom is not through a misunderstanding of China a century old,

44 *Paul Claudel*

but through a recognition of the universality of human aspiration. Now *that* is starting to sound like World Literature.

Although I agree with Damrosch that a work "becomes reframed in its translations and in its new cultural context" (24), he worries me when he claims that it does not matter whether Bei Dao is "superficial in the original," for "(n)ot only is this something that those of us who don't read Chinese cannot judge; it is actually irrelevant to the poem's existence abroad" (22). Of course it matters whether Bei Dao is superficial (or whatever else he might be) in the original, just as it matters how Shakespeare or Dante or James Joyce is in the original. It is difficult to imagine Damrosch cheering on a misreading of Shakespeare just because a Chinese translator gets it wrong, or, worse, wants it to mean something else. To consider the ability to read a text in its original language as mere "leavening of local knowledge" (22) that help the text in translation to rise is to doom the World Literature reader to be like Paul Claudel looking away from the writing that is putatively the object of study in order to admire the color of the walls. We must be careful not to celebrate ignorance pretending to be knowledge simply because we have the power to do so.

Notes

1 By Nakano Shigeharu, translated by Miriam Silverberg, from CHANGING SONG: THE MARXIST MANIFESTOS OF NAKANO SHIGEHARU, translation copyright © 1991 by Miriam Silverberg. Reprinted by permission of Princeton University Press.
2 By Bei Dao, translated by Bonnie S. McDougall, from THE AUGUST SLEEPWALKER, copyright © 1988 by Bei Dao, Translation copyright © 1988, 1990 by Bonnie S. McDougall. Reprinted by permission of New Directions Publishing Corp. Excerpt from "Answer" by Bei Dao, translated by Donald Finkel from A SPLINTERED MIRROR: CHINESE POETRY FROM THE DEMOCRACY MOVEMENT, translated by Donald Finkel. Translation copyright © 1991 by Donald Finkel. Reprinted by permission of North Point Press, a division of Farrar, Strauss and Giroux. According to New Directions Publishing Corp., international copyright beyond North America for the McDougall translation is owned by Carcanet Press. Carcanet did not respond to repeated attempts to reach them.

3 Esteban Echeverría (1805–1851)
La Cautiva Lost to History

Esteban Echeverría's *La Cautiva* (the female captive) is generally understood to be the first work of Argentine Literature, but, to the best of my knowledge, it has never been translated from Spanish into English or any other language. This may simply be because the poem is execrable, perhaps the worst work of literature I've ever read. Even the scholars who write about it don't seem to actually read it, so who could possibly bear to be intimate enough with the poem to translate its 2,135 lines? Perhaps that means it should be excluded from World Literature; its never having been translated bars it from the world, while its utter shittiness may prevent it from being labeled literature. But are these the only two criteria by which to judge a literary work's value?

Many years ago when I held a postdoc at Columbia University, I taught "Lit Hum," one of the core courses required of all Columbia College undergraduates. Literature Humanities was then a Great Works course that began with the Greeks and ended with Virginia Woolf (in 2017 it still began with the Greeks, but now ends with Toni Morrison). There are many odd things about the course, much of them related to the inertia of a core that seems more attuned to the concerns of alumni than the needs of undergraduates: a reliance on dry, inaccurate and outdated translations, intellectual disingenuousness about how knowledge has been transmitted over millennia, a late eighteenth-century Teutonic obsession with Athens to the exclusion of much of the rest of the world, exams that encourage only superficial engagement with the material, and so on. In many ways Lit Hum is the antithesis of World Lit. I nonetheless thought teaching it was great fun and, despite my concerns with the ideological underpinnings of the course, it was an exhilarating and foundational experience that I do not regret.

As a recent PhD poised to become a French professor, I was amused that there was only one book from the French tradition

46 *Esteban Echeverría*

on the Lit Hum reading list, a selection from Montaigne's *Essays*. I have nothing against Montaigne and, in fact, was thrilled to teach the *Essays*, since I thought it unlikely that thereafter I would have many opportunities as a specialist in Francophone (in the narrow sense) Literature to teach it. Fortunately, I was mistaken and have since taught Montaigne several times in various contexts. Nonetheless, just as the *Quijote* had become representative of Hispanophone Literature and *Faust* had become representative of Germanophone Literature in the Lit Hum of my day, so too the *Essays* had become representative of Francophone (here in its broadest sense) Literature. The Italians get Boccacio and Dante, and the Greeks, well, an awful lot, basically 40% of the year-long course. Since many Columbia undergraduates, probably most of them, will never read another work of literature originally written in French,[1] was I sure that Montaigne was the sole Frenchman they should read? Shouldn't undergraduates read, for example, Racine's sublime tragedies, which had moved me to tears of awe when I read them in a survey of French Literature as an undergraduate? Unfortunately, the haunting beauty of his perfectly balanced couplets is lost in translation. What about Camus's *The Stranger*? Most first-year students, at least the Americans, probably read it in high school, which is why Existentialism is all they know about France (plus French bread and *laissez le bon temps rouler*, if they've been to New Orleans). Perhaps they should read some excerpts from Proust? Although some anglophone readers inexplicably claim that Proust is better in English (or, at least, more Proustian www.the-tls.co.uk/articles/private/letters-to-the-editor-november-7-2014/), it is hard to imagine keeping antsy 18-year-olds riveted on the maunders of *Du côté de chez Swann*. The problem for the Great Works instructor cobbling together a syllabus is that there is no French writer akin to Shakespeare in English or Cervantes in Spanish or even Goethe in German. There is probably still a general but fraying consensus that if a student were to read only one author in English that would be Shakespeare, ditto for Cervantes and maybe for Goethe. But still the question remains: what if the student is to read only one author from the French tradition? Hugo? I suppose undergrads can sit through the interminable *Les Miz* on Broadway in lieu of reading *Les Misérables* (or watch the movie on Netflix). Baudelaire? Some of the prose poems seem particularly well-suited to students for whom adolescence is not a distant memory, but it is the poetry that is most remarkable for its adherence to traditional French forms in contrast to the utter modernity of its imagery. Baudelaire's genius is to make

Esteban Echeverría 47

it seem as if all French poetry preceding him leads to him, while all that comes after is in his debt. Since Baudelaire has influenced virtually every self-consciously modern poet of the past 150 years, it might not be a bad idea to assign some of his poems, but they would, unfortunately, make little sense squeezed in between *Pride and Prejudice* and Dostoevsky. Montaigne it must be then.

The problem of representation becomes more acute when the teacher (or fractious committee) organizing the syllabus of an introductory Lit course turns from France to, say, Argentina. No Argentine writer appears on the Lit Hum reading list. And yet Jorge Luis Borges (1899–1986) has, on occasion, made his way into the Lit Hum classroom of individual instructors who make one or the other of his short stories her "free choice" text from the nineteenth or twentieth century, although Borges might lose out to Joyce, Conrad (gasp), or, more to the point, Walcott or García Marquez, according to an official history of the course (www.college.columbia.edu/core/1937.php). I am not arguing that Lit Hum should make all Columbia College undergraduates read some work from Argentine Literature (or any particular work at all, for that matter), but if they must read eight Greek texts, maybe one Latin American text would not be excessive. Should that one be Borges? And if Lit Hum added Borges would they then have to eject Cervantes? I am glad not to confront that choice.

This chapter is not about Borges, but it is impossible to write in English about Argentine Literature without saying *something* about Borges, but exactly which Borges should be trotted out?: the Borges who might round out the twentieth century for Columbia undergrads in Lit Hum, the Borges who makes it into the Norton and Longman anthologies, the Borges of Latin American Literature, or the Borges of Argentine Literature? Just as the great accomplishment of the title character from his famous short story "Pierre Menard, autor del *Quijote*" (Pierre Menard, author of the Quijote) is to write a version of a few selections of the canonical text exactly as Cervantes did, and yet have it mean something else altogether, no Borges text means in precisely the same way once its context has been shuffled. Borges — and the Borgesian text — appears radically different when shifted from one category to the next. This may seem like an obvious and pointless observation, but when I read Borges in Spanish and in Buenos Aires for the first time (and I want to insist that these two experiences are not necessarily identical, since one can read Borges in Spanish anywhere), it was clear to me that this was an author altogether different from the anthologized, translated, de-Argentinized version I'd encountered in years past.

48 *Esteban Echeverría*

World Lit Borges is playful and clever, full of paradox and ample in pluricultural references. Those texts anthologized do not require any footnotes to explain odd *argentinismos* or details of Argentine History that might trip up the reader from elsewhere, because they make no overt reference to anything Argentine. Much like Steven Owens's version of Bei Dao, World Lit Borges is ready-made for translation, already seems to belong to World rather than some national literature. In the Longman *Anthology of World Literature*, for example, Borges is represented by four short stories (from the 1940s) and a poem (published in Spanish in 1980, translated into English in 1986). In "The Garden of Forking Paths" (El jardín de senderos que se bifurcan), "The Library of Babel" (La Biblioteca de Babel), "Borges and I" (Borges y yo), and "Cult of the Phoenix" (La Secta del phénix), there is but one reference to anything Argentine ("Borges and I" refers to Buenos Aires at one point). The late poem "The Web" (La Trama) mentions Buenos Aires, but apparently only to vindicate Borges's decision to die and be buried not there but instead in Geneva. Apparently this was so shocking to Porteños that there was even widespread gossip suggesting that the poem was written not by Borges, but instead by his widow in order to justify spiriting him away to Switzerland at the end of his life (Taranpolsky, n.p.). "The Web" was published a few weeks before his death in English translation in the *New Yorker* and was difficult to find in the original Spanish until reprinted in a bilingual anthology in 2000, so to some degree it has become more an English-language poem than a Spanish-language poem. In all five anthologized works Borges comes off as naturally anglophone as his English grandmother, which is bizarre for a hispanophone writer.

It would be possible, however, to make World Lit Borges into Argentine Lit Borges by choosing equally complex and perplexing short stories that reflect on Argentine history and culture, such as "Funes, el memorioso" (Funes, the memorious) or "El Guerrero y la cautiva" (The warrior and the captive maiden). It would not be difficult to find early Borges poems that consciously Argentinize poetic language and treat Argentine themes, such as the 1925 "El General Quiroga va en coche al muerte..." (General Quiroga takes a carriage to his death), which has also been translated into English. This is not to say that the anthologist who chooses otherwise chooses badly or unwisely, but that he has created for his English-speaking reader one particular Borges rather than another. Reading Borges stories, poems and, especially, criticism focused on Argentina might also cause one to reconsider the vaunted universality of the other texts by Borges. In "The Garden of Forking Paths," for example, a Chinese spying for the Germans in Britain rejects the notion that he has any real sympathy for the Kaiser's German: "nada me importa un país bárbaro" (a barbaric country means nothing at all to me) (Borges, 1996, 473). A bit later in the story an English character refers to himself (in comparison to the Chinese) as a "bárbaro inglés" (English barbarian) (Borges, 1996, 476). That "bárbaro" is applied to both sides of the war is a reminder of the long-running Argentine discourse distinguishing the barbarian from the civilized. Considering Borges's many pronouncements on and explorations of the topic (including in "The Warrior and the captive maiden"), the reference is glaring — unless one has read only international World Lit Borges and therefore cannot perceive any shadow of Argentina crossing the page.

Even "Pierre Menard, el autor del *Quijote*," which seems to be about a Frenchman writing anew the famous Cervantes novel, can also be understood as making some comment on the history of Argentine Literature, although there is no reference whatsoever to anything Argentine in the short story. As I have already pointed out above, the *Quijote* is the Spanish text par excellence, the very epitome of literature in the language shared by its author Cervantes and Borges. "Pierre Menard, el autor del *Quijote*" is a fictional memorial to a deceased minor French symbolist poet and critic/scholar who took it upon himself to write a work that coincided in every way with Cervantes's *Quijote*. Borges mocks the pretentions of academics with his make-believe list of Menard's accomplishments that reads like an annotated CV. But why must Menard be French? Why doesn't Borges conjure up a German philologist or an American close-reader to manufacture a *Quijote* identical in word but radically different in effect?

In "El Aleph" (A Borges narrative not in the aforementioned World Lit anthologies) a narrator who stands in for Borges describes an encounter with Carlos Argentino Daneri, an Argentine poet of sorts, a bit too Italian immigrant for the narrator's taste, who is working on what he believes is his masterpiece, *La Tierra* (The earth). This grand poem intends to encompass everything on the planet. At the narrator's urging he reads a stanza:

He visto, como el griego, las urbes de los hombres,
los trabajos, los días de varia luz, el hambre;
no corrijo los hechos, no falseo los nombres,
pero el *voyage* que narro, es... *autour de ma chambre.*

50   *Esteban Echeverría*

I've seen, like the Greek, the cities of men,
the works, the days of varying light, hunger;
I don't correct the facts or falsify the names,
but the *voyage* I narrate is... *autour de ma chambre*. (Borges,
1996, 619)

Argentino apparently believes that Spanish is not quite the true
language of poetry, so that in his poem it gives way to a butchered
French. However, the grisly last line only rhymes with the second
if the French *chambre* is pronounced as if it were a Spanish word
instead. A Spanish-speaking Italian-origin Argentine poet trying
to heighten his verse with French pronounced as if it were Spanish is ridiculous, just as a French academic trying to write a novel
that coincides in every way with the *Quijote* is absurd. Of course,
it is not impossible for an Argentine to write in French; Hector
Bianciotti (1930–2012) not only wrote novels in French for three decades, but was even elected to the Académie Française. Eduarda
Mansilla (1834–1892) wrote her first novel *Pablo ou la vie dans les
pampas* (Pablo or life on the Pampa) in French. Published in Paris
in 1869, it was also the first novel about the *gaucho*. Her brother,
Lucio Mansilla (1831–1913) did not write in French, but his *Una ex-
cursión a los indios ranqueles* (A journey to the Ranquel Indians), an
account of a journey among a tribe of Indians shortly before they
were exterminated, is written in a Spanish so heavily influenced by
French that it often reads like French written with Spanish words.

I can reach yet further back into the history of Argentina, nearly
to its beginnings as an independent nation. In 1837, Juan María
Gutiérrez (1809–1878) proposed that French be made the national
language of Argentina, as a way of avoiding Spanish cultural subju-
gation (Jitrik, 2005, 31). Although Gutiérrez failed to convince the
other intellectuals of the 1837 Generation to abandon Spanish for
French, their collective Francophilia nonetheless would continue
to influence Argentine Literature for another century at least, if for
no other reason than their being "afrancesado" (Frenchified) made
exile imperative in 1838 when the French navy blockaded the River
Plate (Mercado, 78). Gutiérrez may not have brought about a new
literature in French in Latin America, but he would still be responsible for a reordering of the origins of Argentine national literature
some three decades later, as I will explain shortly.

The question of what exactly is the founding text of Argentine
Literature is fraught with ideological difficulty and historical un-
certainty. As Carlos Gamerro demonstrates in his magisterial

Facundo *o* Martín Fierro. *Los libros que inventaron la Argentina* (Facundo or Martín Fierro. The books that invented Argentina), since at least the lectures of the critic Leopoldo Lugones (1874–1938) just over a century ago, Argentine intellectuals have argued whether Sarmiento's 1845 *Facundo o civilización y barbarie en las pampas argentinas* (Facundo or civilization and barbarism on the Argentine pampa) or José Hernández's 1871 *Martín Fierro* is the nation's founding text (Gamerro, 11). Domingo Faustino Sarmiento (1811–1888), who would later go on to become the most influential Argentine president of all time, wrote his narrative while living in exile in Santiago, the capital of neighboring Chile. In it he condemns the *gaucho* as emblematic of all that is wrong with Argentina, especially its backwardness and violence. José Hernández (1834–1886) twenty-five years later writes *Martín Fierro*, a long poem that makes the long-suffering *gaucho* a sympathetic and Romantic figure. In lectures that were later published as *El Payador*[2] in 1916, Lugones seizes on *Martín Fierro* "after three decades of almost complete neglect" to remake the *gaucho* into an epic figure "within a Homeric frame" (Sorenson, 153). The *gaucho*'s change in fortune was in part due to his disappearance from any role beyond that of a hired farm hand once the final extermination of the native peoples of the Pampa had been completed; he no longer posed any real threat of resistance once the frontier disappeared. In addition, the *gaucho* represented Argentina before the arrival of vast numbers of immigrants from Italy and Spain between 1880 and 1930; by 1900 "immigrants made up 50% of the population of Buenos Aires" (Sorenson, 144). Gamerro sees both works as essential to the foundation of Argentina in its glorious contradiction: "Si *Martín Fierro* fuera, como propone Lugones, nuestra epopeya nacional, *Facundo* sería nuestro Libro del Génesis" (If *Martín Fierro* were, as Lugones proposes, our national epic, *Facundo* would be our Book of Genesis) (Gamerro, 20).

It is, however, possible to imagine other texts as the foundation of Argentine Literature: the first novel, *Amalia*, the initial part of which was published in serial form in Montevideo in 1844, only to be completed in 1851; "El Matadero," often understood as the first Latin American short story, written some time between 1838 and 1840, but not published until 1870; and *La Cautiva*, an epic poem published in 1840, but first read aloud before an audience in 1837. It is not insignificant that each of these works is marked by a complex relationship between composition, reading, and publication, in large part due to the unsettled political

52   Esteban Echeverría

situation in Argentina during the first half of the nineteenth century. Both the author of *Amalia*, José Mármol, and the author of "El Matadero" and *La Cautiva*, Esteban Echeverría, spent much of their adult lives in exile in Uruguay, just as Sarmiento spent much of his adult life in exile in Chile, and Argentine writers of the twentieth century, such as Juan José Saer (1937–2005), spent much of their adult lives in exile in France, Spain or Mexico. *Amalia* is a Romantic novel full of heroism, political intrigue and a love story, but I have not yet come across a critic eager to champion it as the foundation of Argentine Literature. Since *La Cautiva* and "El Matadero" were both written by Echeverría, he would seem to be in competition with himself for the title of founder of Argentine Literature.

To today's World Lit reader "El Matadero" may seem as accomplished and modern as *La Cautiva* seems lousy and dated. If Borges (and Ocampo and Cortázar and many others) made the short narrative the preeminent genre of Argentine Literature, then "El Matadero" is certainly the precursor that heralds them. "El Matadero" begins by rejecting an old-fashioned way of telling stories, the way the colonial Spanish of his time always begins with Noah's ark (Echeverría, 2009, 91). Echeverría sets the scene for the terrible event to come with a description of a city's populace that has gone without meat, a staple of the Argentine diet then as now, during a Lent prolonged by torrential rains that prevented the provisioning of the slaughterhouse on the outskirts of the city (the "matadero" of the title).[3] The reader comes to understand through a series of barbed references to Juan Manuel de Rosas, a federalist dictator called "El Restaurador de leyes" (The restorer of laws) from whose regime Echeverría fled to Uruguay in 1841, that the slaughterhouse represents Argentina itself, led by

> ...el juez del matadero, personaje importante, caudillo de los carniceros y que ejerce la suma del poder en aquella pequeña república por delegación del Restaurador. (Echeverría, 2009, 99)

> ...the judge of the slaughterhouse, an important personage, leader of the butchers and who exercized all power in this little republic through his appointment by the Restorer.

There follows a description of the chaos of the slaughterhouse, with blood-covered butchers hacking at the carcasses while an unpleasant *chusma* (rabble) waits impatiently for scraps. The scene is grotesque with black women throwing mud and offal at each other, slipping and falling in the muck of the slaughterhouse. The threat of mayhem escalates until there is only one animal left to be slaughtered. In the frenzy surrounding it a boy is decapitated, which the *chusma* hardly pauses to note. The steer escapes and as it runs away startles a horse from which an Englishman falls. Yet all this is mere preparation for the shocking confrontation that ends the narrative.

With nothing left to slaughter, one of the butchers calls out that a "unitario" is coming. The Unitarians were the opposition party, to which Echeverría belonged (as did Sarmiento and Mármol, indeed more or less all the writers and intellectuals of the period). He is seized and tied down by the *chusma*. The violence escalates as they berate him for not wearing Federalist insignia and cut his hair with animal shears to make him look more Federalist. And then the fatal words are pronounced by Matasiete ("killed seven"), the leader of the slaughterhouse mentioned above. I know of two translations from the Spanish into English:

> Take the pants off this arrogant fool and beat him on his naked ass. (Echeverría, 1959, 33)

> Take down this foppish dandy's breeches and give his buttock a taste of the rod. (Echeverría, 2010, 30)

They then turn him face down and tie his hands behind his back. The Spanish reads:

> Abajo los calzones a ese cajetilla y a nalga pelada denle verga. (Echeverría, 2009, 113)

I would translate literally and awkwardly as follows, keeping in mind that while *cajeta* means "caramel" in Mexico (which is *dulce de leche* elsewhere in the Spanish-speaking world) it means something else altogether in today's Argentina:

> Drop the panties of this little pussy and give him the rod on his stripped buttock.

In other words, he calls on them to rape him as they would a woman, since "verga" (rod) is a common euphemism for penis in Spanish.

What does it mean that a candidate for the founding text of Argentine Literature ends with a call to homosexual rape (and that

54   Esteban Echeverría

it "is reputed to be the most widely studied school text in all Spanish America" (Echeverría, 2010, xxiv))? The text does not indicate that the rape is committed, since the Unitarian dies, apparently of a burst blood vessel due to his rage, before any one of the bystanders can heed this call to violate him. With his death their fury abates. One of them says that they just wanted to have fun with him but he took it too seriously, which seems disingenuous at best (Echeverría, 2009, 114). One of the most interesting aspects of "El Matadero" is the portrait of this *chusma*, which expresses itself with vocabulary that marks Rioplatense Spanish to this day: "che" and "vos." The language of the narrator is standard Spanish (i.e. "vosotros"). Since there are no documents written by anyone from this social class from the first half of the nineteenth century, "El Matadero" provides a glimpse into a world of which nearly all trace has disappeared, although it is unlikely that Echeverría intended for anyone to read the narrative this way.

Nonetheless, despite the temptation, it is important not to mistake Echeverría's depiction of the *chusma* as an example of Realism, since as Jitrik points out, when Echeverría wrote "El Matadero" in the 1830s Realism did not yet exist (Jitrik, 1997, 87). Echeverría himself makes clear in the 1837 prolog to *La Cautiva* that

> El verdadero poeta idealiza. Idealizar es sustituir a la tosca e imperfecta realidad de la naturaleza, el vivo trasunto de la acabada y sublime realidad que nuestro espiritu alcanza. (Echeverría, 2009, 118)

> The true poet idealizes. To idealize is to substitute for the coarse and imperfect reality of nature, the vivid reflection of the finished and sublime reality to which our spirit strives.

Nonetheless, in 1871 Gutiérrez in his prolog wants the reader to see the "El Matadero" as realistic:

> El artista contribuye al estudio de la sociedad cuando estampa en el lienzo una escena característica, que transportándonos al lugar y a la época en que pasó, nos hace creer que asistimos a ella y que vivimos con la vida de sus actores. (Gutiérrez, no page)

> The artist contributes to the study of a society when he puts to canvas a characteristic scene, which, transporting us to the place and time where it happened, makes us believe that we, too, are present and that we are living alongside its actors.

For his part, Borges said that "El Matadero" contained a "hallucinatory realism," which is Borges having it both ways (Borges, 2004, 126). One of the reasons "El Matadero's" significance feels fundamentally ungraspable is that it was published so long after its composition that the very terms of Literature had changed. It cannot possibly be realist when composed, but by 1871 it felt almost like a time capsule opened to remind Argentines what their country had been like two generations earlier (except that in 1871 time capsules had not yet been invented).

One of the great mysteries of Argentine Literature is not only why Echeverría never published "El Matadero" during his lifetime, but why he never once mentioned it either. When Juan María Gutiérrez, the 1837 Generation intellectual who had called for French to replace Spanish as the national language of Argentina, was preparing his long-dead friend Echeverría's oeuvre for publication in 1870–1874, he came across or came into possession of the manuscript of "El Matadero," or so the story goes. It was published separately in the magazine *Revista del Río de la Plata* in 1871 and then again in the fifth and final volume of the *Obras completas* in 1874. As Emilio Carilla points out, there is no record that anyone ever saw the original manuscript of "El Matadero" except Gutiérrez himself, as it is not found among Echeverría's extant papers (Carilla, 115). As Carilla also notes, Gutiérrez never mentions "El Matadero" in any of his earlier works about Argentine or Latin American Literature, which suggests that, for whatever reason, he did not possess it or become aware of it until shortly before he prepared it for publication (Carilla, 117–119). There is no particular, pressing reason to go so far as to believe that Gutiérrez fabricated "El Matadero," although Carilla notes that he modified other works that he edited (Carilla, 127). A work of doubtful parentage or collaboration is not disqualified from World Lit — after all, who the hell was Homer? — but it almost feels as if "El Matadero" is the narrative that saves Argentine Literature from *La Cautiva* without completely displacing Echeverría as the first real writer of independent Argentina (or even that of post-independence Latin America). If "El Matadero" did not exist, someone would have had to invent it.

But does Argentine Literature, Latin American Literature or World Literature need saving from *La Cautiva*?

Shittiness in and of itself does not necessarily exclude a work from World Lit. Over and over in essays about World Literature are references to its ur-moment, when in January, 1827 Goethe tells his visitor Johann Peter Eckermann that he has been reading a Chinese novel.

56 *Esteban Echeverría*

He does not mention this "chinesischer Roman" by name, but scholarly consensus, although not in absolute agreement, awards the prize to the no-longer-read seventeenth-century novel 好逑傳 (The Fortunate Union), author unknown (Mani, 285). As Jing Tsu notes, "[t]he Chinese novel, in other words, is more Chinese than it is a novel," and that's why Goethe finds it interesting and useful, regardless of whatever literary value it might have or, in this case, not have (Tsu, 163). Taking a cue from Goethe, one might also argue that *La Cautiva* is more Argentine than poetry; putting aside Echeverría's contemporaries, whose praise was often florid, I have never read a critic who considered the poem's value to lie in its form or execution. Although *The Fortunate Union* is no longer read in English (or Portuguese) translation for its value as literature, if read at all, its omnipresence in histories of *Weltliteratur* must award it an honorary place in World Literature. Although *La Cautiva* was not written by Anonymous, it does have the virtue of mysterious origins and a besmirched manuscript history, so might not it, too, deserve a World Lit slot?

When *La Cautiva* is praised, it is usually for its promise, which strikes me as an unusual way to talk about a work written 180 years ago. Borges, picking his words carefully, praises the *La Cautiva* for "discovering the aesthetic possibilities of the Pampa and nomadic Indians," which suggests that Echeverría's poem has not actually realized any of these aesthetic possibilities (Borges, 2004, 126). This is a not atypical stanza from the first part, "El Desierto" (the desert):

> Sólo a ratos, altanero
> relinchaba un bruto fiero
> aquí o allá, en la campaña;
> bramaba un toro de saña,
> rugía un tigre feroz;
> o las nubes contemplando,
> como extático o gozoso,
> el yajá, de cuando en cuando,
> turbaba el mudo reposo
> con su fatídica voz. (Echeverría, 2009, 127–8)

> Only at times, haughtily
> neighed a ferocious brute
> here or there, in the countryside;
> bellowed a vicious bull,
> roared a fierce tiger;
> or, contemplating the clouds,

Esteban Echeverría   57

whether in ecstasy or joy
the *yajá*, from time to time,
disturbed the mute repose
with his terrible voice.

Having mentioned the silence of this putative desert in the previous stanza, Echeverría offers a contrast with a generalization about the sounds wild animals in the Pampa make, then follows with references to three specific animals and their sounds: a tiger, a bull and a yajá. The tiger is actually a jaguar, since there are no tigers in Argentina and in Latin America the jaguar is called *tigre*. The bull seems to be, well, a bull; if it refers to the adult male of some other sort of animal, Echeverría does not make that clear. These first two animals then are either European or assimilated to European animals. The *yajá* is a bird found on the Pampa. My edition of *La Cautiva* includes a very interesting note about the peculiarities of this bird; indeed, the note is much more interesting than the poem.

Despite what Borges writes, *La Cautiva* has no real interest in pointing toward aesthetic possibilities, but instead misses them altogether, because it has no interest in the landscape of the Pampa or any other real place for that matter. As Cristina Iglesia points out, most literary critics who write about *La Cautiva* get it backward; they believe that the "desierto" of the Pampa gives rise to the poem, but, in fact, it is just a space to which the poem alludes, a "pingüe patrimonio" (a rich patrimony) that Echeverría recognizes, or perhaps even invents for the nation of Argentina after his sojourn in Europe (Iglesia, 5). The poem begins with epigraphs from Byron and Hugo, which remove the reader to the opposite side of the Atlantic before, reluctantly, dragging him back to the Pampa. Despite a few references to the local flora and fauna, including the *ombú* tree that will grow over the graves of the hero and heroine (Echeverría, 2009, 221), I never feel immersed in the scenery as I feel immersed in the slung muck of the slaughterhouse of "El Matadero." This so-called desert is not a place, but instead just a sparsely propped stage for the tragedy of Brian and María, a tragedy that never quite manages to fret the reader. The Pampa of *La Cautiva* feels no more real to me than the mountainous wilderness surrounding New Orleans that the imaginative Abbé Prévost (1697–1763) invents for the dénouement of his novel *Manon Lescaut*, which, despite its equally Romantic (or, perhaps better, romantic) sheen, is unlikely to be a model for *La Cautiva*, as only one of the star-crossed lovers dies rather than both. The critic Gonzales Echevarría (no relation), finds beyond the

58 *Esteban Echeverría*

local color of Echeverría's references a "Romantic sublime" emerging from a "feeling of the infinite," in other words, what Echeverría brings back from Romantic Europe to far-off Argentina, not what he finds in Argentina itself (Gonzales Echevarría, 17). That said, it was no small feat to be the bearer of Romanticism to an entire continent and for that Echeverría should be recognized.

The plot of *La Cautiva* is not only odd, but weirdly free of tension, surprise and suspense. Leaving aside the depiction of the Indians in part two, which is unleavened by any ethnographic detail that might place them beyond the generalities of babarity, the plot begins with María returning from her own escape to rescue her counterpart Brian. I have never understood why Echeverría chose Brian as his *cautivo*'s name. It certainly was not because it is easy to rhyme in Spanish. Indeed, when Brian first appears in the poem, his name is made to rhyme with Quillán and Callupán, suggesting that Echeverría had to invent Indian-sounding names to line up with Brian (which should be Brián) (Echeverría, 2009, 140). Fortunately, María is much easier to rhyme, with words such as *fantasía, esparcía, fría* (Echeverría, 2009, 154, 202, 206). Unfortunately, Echeverría botches her entrance:

> Silencio; ya el paso leve
> por entre la yerba mueve,
> como quien busca y no atina,
> y temeroso camina
> de ser visto o tropezar,
> una mujer; en la diestra
> un puñal sangriento muestra,
> sus largos cabellos flotan
> desgreñados, y denotan
> de su ánimo el batallar. (Echeverría, 2009, 150)

> Silence; already a delicate step
> moves through the grass,
> like someone who searches to no avail,
> and walks fearful
> of being seen or stumbling,
> a woman; in her right hand
> a bloody dagger shows,
> her long hair floats
> disheveled, yet denotes
> the fight in her spirit.

Esteban Echeverría 59

The stanza wants to build suspense about just who is moving through the grass by moving the subject of the sentence to the sixth line, but because the adjectives "temeroso" (fearful) and "visto" (seen) must agree in gender with "quien" (someone, neither male nor female, and therefore grammatically masculine) rather than "mujer" (woman, and therefore grammatically female), the reader stumbles while trying to figure out who is stumbling.

It would be easy to catalog a list of *La Cautiva*'s sins against Literature, World or otherwise, and against common sense, but I will simply point out that the potential thrill of María's heroism is marred by its expression, its unfortunate choice of object, and its failure. She dispatches an Indian with her dagger so quickly that the murder hardly registers, especially since Brian's reaction to her act of heroism is unchivalrous at best: "María, soy infelice, / ya no eres digna de mi" (María, I am unhappy, / already you are no longer worthy of me) (Echeverría, 2009, 155). The reader might wonder why she bothers to cut him loose and drag him through the desert after that. She lets him know with a wave of her dagger and a little speech that she let the savage have it when he tried to outrage her honor, although she was too late to save their child. Echeverría seems to forget that María has already told Brian this when the topic of the dead child comes up again later. In any case, for a warrior Brian is oddly defeatist and whiny. His death is a relief, and not just for Brian himself.

A work like *La Cautiva* would seem to be inadmissible to World Literature not just because it is shitty poetry (and that it is), but because the ideas it expresses, insofar as it expresses any, run counter to the "We Are the World" ethos of World Lit. The text is about division, exclusion and, eventually, extermination. Indeed, "Argentina is the only country in Latin America that has determinedly and successfully erased the mestizo, Indian, and black minorities from its history and reality" (Rotker, 20).[4] Since World Lit is about the American reader (in this case American as in *estadounidense*, since Argentines are also American), perhaps it would be useful for us (them?) to read a work that initiates genocides more successful than our/their own. Putting aside the parallels between Argentine and *estadounidense* history, when put into an even larger context, the slack verse, irritating rhymes, imagery masquerading as local color and absurd characters of *La Cautiva* are not without value. There are some works of the human imagination that somehow manage to be beautiful, despite their heinous message. Leni Riefenstal's *Triumph des Willens* (Triumph of the Will) is breathtaking, but

60 *Esteban Echeverría*

its glorification of fascism is vile. D.W. Griffith's *Birth of a Nation* marks the culmination of a revolution in cinematic technique, but its depiction of black men is sickening. The music of *Madama Butterfly* is sublime, but its depiction of the self-sacrificing Asian woman is loathsome. In this company the aesthetic failure of *La Cautiva* is a relief; finally a work that lives down to its ideology. Perhaps the coincidence of incompetent authorship and odious ideology should not exclude *La Cautiva* from World Literature, but should instead guarantee its entry, since it marks the perfect union of the unaesthetic with the unethical.

Notes

1 Columbia undergraduates read selections from Descartes, Rousseau, Toqueville, Fanon and Foucault in "Contemporary Civilization" or CC, but since Rousseau was Swiss, Toqueville wrote about America, and Fanon and Foucault have been so assimilated into the American academy that they hardly qualify as French-language writers any more, these writers function as more universal than French on this reading list. Rabelais, Molière and Voltaire have popped on and off the Lit Hum reading list in ages past (https://www.college.columbia.edu/core/1937. php), but Montaigne is the only French writer to never disappear from it.
2 A *payador* is a singer of *payada*s, an improvised song sung in competition with another *payador*.
3 As Jitrik points out, Echeverría has just said he would *not* start with Noah's Ark and then he recounts a story of "una inundación" (a flood) (Jitrik, 1997, 68).
4 Rotker overstates her case. There are mestizos and even indigenous people in Argentina beyond Buenos Aires and the Pampa.

4 Jamīl Buthayna (7th c.) in the *Book of Songs* (10th c.)

Man out of Poetry

Since the Arab tradition of lyric poetry is among the world's richest and oldest, with an unbroken history of at least 1,500 years, it would be foolhardy to construct a model of World Literature that somehow excludes it. Within this tradition Jamīl may very well be the single most influential of its great many poets. Unfortunately, however, none of his poems survive. Although it might seem beyond the talents of even the most gifted and dedicated scholar to make known to the World Lit reader nonexistent works, happily this is not the case. In the 1930s the influential Italian orientalist Francesco Gabrieli (1904–1996) made up his mind to reconstruct Jamīl's *dīwān* (the Arabic term for a book containing much if not all of an individual poet's work), parts of which he also translated into Italian. While the goal was no doubt laudable, what he did instead was create a book that most likely never before existed, full of poems that were most likely never composed, whether by Jamīl or by anyone else. It may be the case that none of the individual lines of poetry cobbled together to form these "poems" are Jamīl's either. I want to make the case that a fundamental misunderstanding of where Jamīl's genre appeal lies has obscured his value to both Arabic Literature and World Literature. The imposition of a European idea of what a poem is has distorted Arabic Literature by creating an entirely new book that is then assigned ancient provenance. Unfortunately, the longest of these "poems" by Jamīl are now so incoherent that they give today's reader little, and at most, sporadic pleasure. At the same time, the misidentification of the Jamīl narrative of the eleventh-century *Kitāb al-Aghānī* (Book of Songs) as merely a compendium of information in which the individual lines of poetry assigned to Jamīl have been embedded (and thereby saved for posterity) rather than as a complex literary text in its own right further complicates any attempt to understand just what Jamīl, or, perhaps better, "Jamīl" as a category of Arabic verse, means. Because Gabrieli's *dīwān* has

62   Jamīl Buthayna

been vastly influential in the Arab world as well, in this case Western scholarship has remade Arabic Literature and its understanding of itself, and, I fear, not for the better.

As I have already written extensively on Gabrieli's putative reconstruction of Jamīl's *dīwān*, I will summarize that part of my argument here and then focus on the narratives in the *Book of Songs*.[1] Little is known about Jamīl's life. He is said to have been born in the Hijaz, the westernmost region of the Arabian Peninsula, about 660 C.E., so roughly a generation and a half after the death of the Prophet Muḥammad. What virtually every literate Arab knows about Jamīl is that he falls in love with his cousin Buthayna, such that he is often simply called "Jamīl Buthayna" (which means "Buthayna's Jamīl" or "Jamīl of Buthayna"). Displeased, her family marries her off to another man. Jamil's suffering that results which unleashes poem after poem after poem. Jamīl was not alone in writing such tormented love poetry; he was an 'Udhrī, a tribe known for its many poets dying for love that could not be. The poetry of these other 'Udhrīs is also fragmentary and mostly lost, although to the best of my knowledge only Jamīl's *dīwān* has been subjected to an attempted reconstruction. What the poetry ascribed to Jamīl makes new is the relationship between the enamored poet and the beloved. In pre-Islamic poetry, the poet — any poet — famously struggles to recall the site where he knew a beloved woman briefly as their transhumant tribes crossed paths. When many years later he comes across some sign in the desert of the traces of her tribe's abandoned encampments, a flood of memories is unleashed. In contrast, Jamīl and the other 'Udhrī poets do not suffer from any difficulty in remembering. Instead, each remembers incessantly the beloved woman from whom he has been permanently separated. In both cases, pre-Islamic and 'Udhrī, the woman herself is of little importance. In the case of pre-Islamic poets the man's erotic adventure is an occasion to demonstrate his lyric prowess in fulfilling the genre demands of the form. In the case of the 'Udhrī poets, it is the expression of the despairing and obsessive feelings that the unreachable beloved inspires that matter.

Gabrieli's constructions further muddle things. Since he assembles all the longer poems with lines from so many different sources, the characterization of Buthayna seems to whipsaw from one sort of woman to another from one line to the next. The longest of his constructions, the poem he numbers #27, is made up of 39 lines taken from twelve sources dating from the ninth to sixteenth centuries. I have indicated in italics within brackets various Arabic words that might be translated into English as "love," although

I have endeavored to find some more specific English words to represent each of them (Gabrieli, 69).

١	أَلَا لَيْتَ رَيْعَانَ ٱلشَّبَابِ جَدِيد	وَدَهْرًا تَوَلَّى يَا بُثَيْنَ يَعُود
٢	فَنَغْنَى كَمَا كُنَّا نَكُونُ وَأَنْتُمْ	صَدِيقٌ وَإِنْ مَا تَبْذُلِينَ زَهِيد
٣	وَمَا أَنْسَ مَلْأَشْيَاءَ لَا أَنْسَ قَوْلَها	وَقَدْ قَرَّبَتْ نَضْوِى أَمِصْرَ تُرِيد
٤	وَلَا قَوْلَها لَوْلَا ٱلْعُيُونُ ٱلَّتِي تَرَى	أَتَيْتُكَ فَٱعْذِرْنِى فَدَتْكَ جُدُود
٥	خَلِيلَيَ مَا أُخْفِي مِنَ ٱلْوَجْدِ ظَاهِرٌ	دَمْعِى بِمَا أُخْفِى ٱلْغَدَاةَ شَهِيد
٦	أَلَا قَدْ أَرَى وَٱللهِ أَنْ رُبَّ عَبْرَةٍ	إِذَا ٱلدَّارُ شَطَّتْ بَيْنَنا سَتَزِيد
٧	إِذَا قُلْتُ مَا بِى يَا بُثَيْنَةُ قَاتِلِي	مِنَ ٱلْوَجْدِ قَالَتْ ثَابِتٌ وَيَزِيد
٨	وَإِنْ قُلْتُ رُدِّى بَعْضَ عَقْلِ أَعِشْ بِهِ	مَعَ ٱلنَّاسِ قَالَتْ ذَاكَ مِنْكَ بَعِيد
٩	فَلَا أَنَا مَرْدُودٌ بِمَا جِئْتُ طَالِبًا	وَلَا حُبُّهَا فِيمَا يَبِيدُ يَبِيد
١٠	جَزَتْكِ ٱلْجَوَازِى يَا بُثَيْنَ مَلَامَةً	إِذَا مَا خَلِيلٌ بَانَ وَهْوَ حَمِيد
١١	وَقُلْتُ لَهَا بَيْنِى وَبَيْنَكِ فَٱعْلَمِي	مِنَ ٱللهِ مِيثَاقٌ لَهُ وَعُهُود
١٢	وَقَدْ كَانَ حُبَيْكُمْ طَرِيفًا وَتَالِدًا	مَا ٱلْحُبُّ إِلَّا طَارِفٌ وَتَلِيد
١٣	وَإِنَّ عُرُوضَ ٱلْوَصْلِ بَيْنِى وَبَيْنَهَا	وَإِنْ سَهَّلَتْهُ بِالْمُنَى لَصَعُود
١٤	فَأَفْنَيْتُ عَيْشِى بِٱنْتِظَارِى نَوَالَهَا	وَأَبْلَيْتُ أَكَ ٱلدَّهْرَ وَهْوَ جَدِيد
١٥	فَلَيْتَ وُشَاةَ ٱلنَّاسِ بَيْنِى وَبَيْنَهَا	يَذُوفُ لَهُمْ سُمًّا طَمَاطِمُ سُود
١٦	وَلَيْتَ لَهُمْ فِى كُلِّ مُمْسًى وَشَارِقٍ	وَضَاعَفَ أَكْبَالٌ لَهُمْ وَقُيُود
١٧	وَيَحْسِبُ نِسْوَانٌ مِنَ ٱلْجَهْلِ أَنَّنِى	إِذَا جِئْتُ إِيَّاهُنَّ كُنْتُ أُرِيد
١٨	فَأَقْسِمُ طَرْفِى بَيْنَهُنَّ فَيَسْتَوِى	وَفِى ٱلصَّدْرِ بَوْنٌ بَيْنَهُنَّ وَبَعِيد
١٩	أَلَا لَيْتَ شِعْرِى هَلْ أَبِيتَنَّ لَيْلَةً	بِوَادِى ٱلْقُرَى إِنِّى إِذًا لَسَعِيد
٢٠	وَهَلْ أَهْبِطَنْ أَرْضًا تَظَلُّ رِيَاحَها	لَهَا بِالثَّنَايَا ٱلْقَاوِيَاتِ وَئِيد
٢١	وَهَلْ أَلْقَيَنْ سَعْدَى مِنَ ٱلدَّهْرِ مَرَّةً	وَمَا رَثَّ مِنْ حَبْلِ ٱلصَّفَاءِ جَدِيد
٢٢	وَقَدْ تَلْتَقِى ٱلْأَهْوَاءُ مِنْ بَعْدِ يَأْسَةٍ	وَقَدْ تُطْلَبُ ٱلْحَاجَاتُ وَهْىَ بَعِيد
٢٣	وَهَلْ أَزْجُرَنْ حَرْفًا عَلَاةً شِمْلَةً	بِخَرْقٍ تُبَارِيها سَوَاهِمْ قُود
٢٤	عَلَى ظَهْرِ مَرْهُوبٍ كَأَنَّ نُشُوزَه	إِذَا جَازَ هُلَّاكَ ٱلطَّرِيقِ رُقُود
٢٥	سَبَتْنِى بِعَيْنَىْ جُؤْذَرٍ وَسْطَ رَبْرَبِ	وَصَدْرٍ كَفَاثُورِ ٱللُّجَيْنِ وَجِيد
٢٦	تَزِيفُ كَمَا زَافَتْ إِلَى سَلِفَاتِها	مُبَاهِيَةٌ طَىُّ ٱلْوِشَاحِ هَيُود
٢٧	إِذَا جِئْتُها يَوْمًا مِنَ ٱلدَّهْرِ زَائِرًا	تَعَرَّضَ مَنْقُوضُ ٱلْيَدَيْنِ صَدُود
٢٨	يَصُدُّ وَيُغْضِبِى عَنْ هَوَاىَ وَيَجْدَنِى	دُنُو بَاعَلَيْهَا إِنَّهُ لَعَنُود
٢٩	فَأَصْرِمُهَا خَوْفًا كَأَنِى مُجَانِبٌ	وَيَغْفُلُ عَنَّا مَرَّةً فَنَعُود
٣٠	فَمَنْ يُعْطَ فِى ٱلدُّنْيَا قَرِينًا كَمِثْلِهَا	فَذَلِكَ فِى عَيْشِ ٱلْحَيَاةِ رَشِيد
٣١	يَمُوتُ ٱلْهَوَى مِنَّى إِذَا مَا لَقِيتُها	وَيَحْىَ إِذَا فَارَقْتُهَا فَيَعُود
٣٢	يَقُولُونَ جَاهِدْ يَا جَمِيلُ بِغَزْوَةٍ	وَأَىُّ جِهَادٍ غَيْرُهُنَّ أُرِيد
٣٣	لِكُلِّ حَدِيثٍ بَيْنَهُنَّ بَشَاشَةٌ	وَكُلُّ قَتِيلٍ بَيْنَهُنَّ شَهِيد
٣٤	وَمَنْ كَانَ فِى حُبِّى بُثَيْنَة يَمْتَرِى	فَبَرْقَاءُ ذِى ضَالٍ عَلَىَّ شَهِيد
٣٥	أَلَمْ تَعْلَمِى يَا أُمَّ ذِى ٱلْوَدْعِ أَنَّنِى	أُصَاحِكُ ذِكْرَاكُمْ وَأَنْتَ صَلُود
٣٦	عَلِقْتُ ٱلْهَوَى مِنْها وَلِيدًا فَلَمْ يَزَلْ	إِلَى ٱلْيَوْمِ يَنْمِى حُبُّها وَيَزِيد
٣٧	إِذَا فَكَّرَتْ قَالَتْ قَدِ ٱدَّرَكْتُ وُدَّهُ	وَمَا ضَرَّنِى بُخْلٌ كَيْفَ أَجُود
٣٨	فَلَوْ تُكْشَفُ ٱلْأَحْشَاءُ صُودِفَ تَحْتَها	لِبُثْنَةَ حُبٌّ طَارِفٌ وَتَلِيد
٣٩	فَمَا ذُكِرَ ٱلْخُلَّانُ إِلَّا ذَكَرْتُها	وَلَا ٱلْبُخْلُ إِلَّا قُلْتُ سَوْفَ تَجُود

64 *Jamīl Buthayna*

1 If only the first flowering of youth could be renewed,
    and the time that turned and fled, O Buthayna, returned.

2 We could continue on contented as we were,
    you a true friend though you gave me but little.

3 Whatever things I may forget, I will not forget the words she spoke
    when she allowed my worn-out camel near: "To Egypt bound?"

4 Nor her words: "If not for spying eyes,
    I would come to you, so forgive me — may the ancestors ransom you!"

5 O my two friends, the passion [wajd] I hide is obvious;
    my tears are witness to what I hide this morning.

6 Do I not see — God! — that there will be ever more tears
    when the abode puts a great distance between us.

7 When I said, "O Buthayna, the passion [wajd] in me is my murderer,"
    she said, "It will always be so and and only get worse."

8 If I said, Restore but some of my wits so that I may live among people,
    she would say: "Far from it!"

9 I am not sent back with that which I came seeking,
    nor will my love [hubb] for her perish like that which perishes.

10 May they compensate you with reproach, O Buthayna,
    when a praiseworthy friend departs.

11 And I said to her, "Between me and you, know
    that before God we have a pact and vows.

12 My love [hubb] for you is both newfound and long-possessed,
    there being no love [hubb] that is not both newly-gained and won long ago."

13 The mountain path toward union between her and me,
    even if she leveled it with desire [manā], would be steep.

14 I wore out my life waiting for her favor,
    and used up time while it was still new.

15 If only muttering black strangers would mix poison destined
    for the rumor-mongers spreading lies about her and me among the people.

16 If only at every dusk and every dawn
    their shackles and fetters were doubled!

17 Those women imagine out of ignorance
    that when I came I wanted [urīdu] them.

18 I divide my glances equally among the women
    but in my breast the gap between them is vast.

Jamīl Buthayna 65

19 If only I knew whether I would ever spend one night
    at Wād al-Qurā, I would then truly be happy.
20 Will I alight in a land whose winds persist
    howling over abandoned highland paths?
21 And whether I, one fated time, will truly meet with my good
    fortune,
        so that the worn bond of sheer friendship [safā'] will be renewed.
22 Longing loves [plural of hawā] may meet after having despaired;
    what one needs may be sought although far off.
23 Will I drive my lank, tall, swift camel across a wind-swept
    plain
        where the long-necked journey-weary camels try to out-run her
24 Over a feared desert plain, the heights of which are as if
    sleeping when those who will die lost pass by?
25 With the eyes of a wild calf amid a herd,
        and with a breast smooth as a silver plate she took me captive;
26 She walks head held high, the way one vaunting her beauty
    walks, swaying, wearing a jewelled belt, toward her sisters-in-law.
27 When I went to visit her one fateful day,
        a man untwisting his hands showed up to stop me,
28 He turned away and closed his eyes at my longing [hawā], falsely
    charging me with crimes against her, rejecting what he knew
    to be true.
29 So I cut myself off from her out of fear, as if I were avoiding her;
        but when he pays no attention to us, we will return.
30 Whoever is given in this world a wife like her
        will live a life well-led.
31 My longing [hawā] dies when I see her,
    and when I part from her, it revives, returning.
32 The men say, O Jamīl, take up arms and wage holy war!
    but why would I want holy war not waged against women?
33 All talk among women is a joy;
    anyone killed in their midst is a martyr.
34 To whoever doubts my love [hubb] for Buthayna
    let the stone-mottled sands of Dhū Dāl be my witness.
35 Don't you know, o Mother of the cowry-charm, that I laugh
    remembering you, despite your hardness?
36 I was caught by longing [hawā] for her when just a boy, and my
    love [hubb] for her
        has never to this day stopped growing and increasing.
37 Upon reflection she said, "I've already attained his affection [wudd],
    stinginess cannot hurt me, so why should I be generous?"

66   *Jamīl Buthayna*

38 If my guts were laid bare, you would find under them
   my love [*hubb*] for Buthayna — both the newly-gained and
   long-ago won.
39 No friends are remembered without my remembering her
   and no stinginess without my saying, "She will be generous."

The cycling among various somewhat contradictory words to indicate his feelings might indicate the tumult of mad love, except that the very word for mad love, *'ishq*, is missing altogether from this poem. Even less consistent than the poet's feelings is the representation of Buthayna, who in line 2 is accused of being ungenerous (meaning she won't make herself sexually available), while in line 4 she says she would come to him if she could, and then she's stingy again near the end of the poem. A figure already out of focus, because the beloved in this sort of poetry is not meant to be individualized, blurs yet further in this Frankenstein's monster of a poem. In the narratives about Jamīl and Buthayna, however, the latter becomes a three-dimensional character with will and guile.

Where are these narratives found? Compiled by Abū al-Faraj al-Isfahānī (897–967), the *Book of Songs* is not only the single most important source of classical Arabic poetry for scholars, but also includes vast amounts of other sorts of information about singers and performance at the Abbasid court and elsewhere in tenth-century Baghdad. Although some of its lacunae are inexplicable (Abū Nuwās, e.g. is nowhere to be found), it is hard to imagine writing a history of Arabic Literature without it. Far more than a dictionary or encyclopedia, however, the *Book of Songs* also provides sparkling anecdotes that form portraits of many poets. The section on Jamīl may be among the best (although the anecdotes about his contemporary, the drunken Christian poet al-Akhṭal [c. 640–710] are hilarious). Although al-Isfahānī takes these anecdotes from sources that he cites clearly and rigorously, those related to Jamīl are not only in and of themselves deft literary texts, but together form something akin to a short story or even a novella that presents to the cosmopolitan Abbasid reader the arc of the lives of Buthayna and Jamīl. It is important to note the importance, even the centrality, of the anecdote to Arabic Literature broadly conceived. The most important narrative of Arabic Literature, the story of the life of the Prophet Muḥammad, was constructed through the compilation and arrangement of anecdotes about something he said or did that were transmitted orally

Jamīl Buthayna 67

and, later, textually. Indeed, it is difficult to imagine Islam without these *ḥadīths*, since the biographical information they convey is nowhere to be found in the Qur'ān itself, which has virtually nothing to say about Muḥammad. The anecdote then is a valued genre in Arabic Literature, while it is generally considered of little value in Euro-American Literatures. This may help to explain why Gabrieli undertakes to assemble poems by Jamīl in opposition to the work already done by medieval Arabic scholars who chose instead to assemble anecdotes into narratives. The task of World Literature then is not to ignore genres valued by other cultures, but to find a place for them — and to foster understanding of how the construction of genre boundaries and their imposition on non-Euro-American Literatures distorts those literatures.

The section of the *Book of Songs* about Jamīl begins as would a typical entry in any biographical dictionary, with a lengthy explanation of Jamīl's full name followed by his genealogy (both with regard to his family and to his place within a lineage of poets, each of whom has been a transmitter [*rāwiya*] for another poet). This is important for two reasons, first because poetry was at the time transmitted orally, and because Jamīl's transmitter, Kuthayyir (c. 660–723), later a poet in his own right, will be a major character in the ensuing narrative. There is little in this prefatory material, which sticks to the formulae of medieval Arabic biographical notices, to suggest the quality of the anecdotes to come. Nonetheless, despite the pages devoted to this recondite material, it thereafter quickly becomes clear that al-Isfahānī is interested not in the biography of Jamīl *per se*, but instead in the story of Buthayna and Jamīl.

Once his genealogy is established, Jamīl's life before he meets Buthayna is summed up in a brief sentence and then the first of their disturbing encounters is described (*Kitāb al-Aghānī* or *KA*, 293).

> Jamīl had been composing *nasīb*s [a sort of love poem] for Umm al-Jusayr [elsewhere said to be Buthayna's sister]. His devotion to Buthayna began the day that he approached a *wādī* [a usually dry river bed that intermittently carries water] named Baghīẓ to water his camels. He lay down to sleep, letting his camels wander off upstream. Since Buthayna's people were camped at the end of the *wādī*, Buthayna and one of her slave-girls drew near while they were heading to the water. When the

68 *Jamīl Buthayna*

two of them passed the already-weaned camel calves kneeling [presumably to drink], Buthayna was mean to them. It's said that she frightened them off. She and her slave were then just little girls. Jamīl reprimanded her and she insulted him, but her abuse was beautiful to him.[2]

The psychology of the anecdote is already more complex than that of any of the poems cobbled together by Gabrieli. There is no hint of the figure described in the poems in the little girl who goes off with another little girl unaccompanied by any man, shoos away a strange man's camels while they are drinking and, when caught in the act and upbraided, insults him. The result? Jamīl finds her abuse beautiful. Oh my.

Although his perverse emotional reaction to Buthayna's sassiness bodes ill for Jamīl, it is only in the next anecdote, presumably many years later, that he falls in love with her (*KA*, 293).

Jamīl went out on a feast day for which the women had adorned themselves; some of them showed themselves not only to other women but also to men. Jamīl stopped before Buthayna and her sister Umm al-Jusayr among the women of the Banī al-Aḥabb, who were closely related to him, as they were daughters of his father's brother 'Ubayd Allāh ibn Quṭba. He saw among the women one who held his gaze. She astounded him. He fell in love (عشق) with Buthayna and sat with them. When he left as night fell young men of the Banī al-Aḥabb accompanied him. He realized that Buthayna's people had recognized in his gaze his love (حب) for Buthayna and were angry at him.

The verb indicating that he has fallen in love is *'ashiqa*, the very same crazed, helpless love that is missing from Gabrieli's poem and for which Jamīl is famous. The power of the Jamīl and Buthayna narrative is such that whatever there might be in the poetry ascribed to Jamīl that would contradict the love story must be coopted. If Jamīl composed love poems to another woman, then she must be assigned to Buthayna's family, must lead to Buthayna, and must be a Buthayna precursor. The narrative must also find some way for Jamīl to see her and to meet her, for otherwise how could he fall in love with her?

The following is my favorite of all the anecdotes. In it ever-lovesick Jamīl prevails upon his transmitter and friend Kuthayyir to return to Buthayna's family to arrange a tryst, although he has just left, while Buthayna manages to convey a secret message to Jamīl (*KA*, 299–300).

Kuthayyir sat down with us one day and we reminisced about Jamīl. He said, Once he ran into me and asked where I was coming from. "From the father of the beloved" (meaning Buthayna), he replied. He said, "So where are you going?" I replied, "To the beloved" (meaning 'Azza [his own beloved]). Jamīl said, "You must go back where you've just come from and again try to arrange a tryst with Buthayna for me." I replied, "But I just saw her. I would blush with shame if I went back so soon." He said, "You have to." I asked him, "When did you last meet with Buthayna?" "At the beginning of the summer," he replied, A rain-cloud had stopped at the bottom of the Wādī al-Daum, so she went out accompanied by one of her slave-girls to wash her laundry. When she saw me she did not recognize me, and so reached with her hand for the laundry in the water to cover herself with it; but the slave-girl knew who I was and put the laundry back in the water. We talked until the sun set. I asked to see her again and she replied, "My people are traveling." I haven't found anyone I trust to send to her. Then Kuthayyir asked him, "So how about if I went to her clan and tossed out a few lines of a poem by which I make known to her some sign, in case I am unable to meet with her in private?" He replied, "That would be the right thing to do," and sent him to her. Kuthayyir said, "So wait for me," and he set out until he reached them. Her [Buthayna's] father asked him, "Why have you come back?" Kuthayyir replied, "Three lines of poetry came to me and I wanted to recite them to you." He said, "Let's have them!" Kuthayyir said, I recited them to him while Buthayna listened in:

I said, O 'Azza, my companion is sent to you, a messenger to whom a message has been entrusted,
To arrange between you and me a tryst, doing on my behalf that which I would do;
The last time I saw you was the day you met me at the bottom of Wādī al-Daum while washing your clothes.

Then Buthayna struck the side of her tent and shouted, "Scram! Scram!" Her father said, "What's wrong, Buthayna?" She replied, "There's a dog that comes around from behind that hill when people are sleeping." Then she said to her slave-girl,

70   *Jamīl Buthayna*

"We should gather some firewood at al-Dawmāt. Let's slaughter a sheep for Kuthayyir and roast it for him." But Kuthayyir said, "I'm in too much of a hurry for that!" and rushed back to Jamīl to report to him. Jamīl said, "So the tryst will be at al-Dawmāt." In the meantime Buthayna spoke to her cousins Umm al-Ḥusayn, Lailā and Nujayyā, to whom she'd grown close, and with whom she was at ease: "I saw in Kuthayyir's recitation that Jamīl had been with him." Kuthayyir and Jamīl set out until they reached al-Dawmāt. Then Buthayna and those who accompanied her arrived. They departed only when the sun rose. Kuthayyir used to say, "I never saw a gathering more beautiful than this, nor anything like the knowledge of the innermost soul that one had for the other. I do not know which of the two better understood the other!"

The anecdote has done World Literature no favor by preserving the three lines of doggerel by Kuthayyir, if they are indeed his. The poet may be fortunate that Buthayna makes a ruckus with "Scram! Scram!" otherwise her father might have offered some scathing literary criticism or some pointed question as to why these lines required immediate transmission.

The interest of the anecdote lies not with the preserved verse but in the complexity of the prose (try building a *dīwān* of Kuthayyir around those three lines). The very structure of the anecdote seems to insist on how contagious longing is. Here Kuthayyir is a character who misses Jamīl and therefore tells a story in which Jamīl misses Buthayna and therefore tells a story about her. It is implied that Buthayna then tells the story of Kuthayyir's visit on behalf of Jamīl to her cousins. And, finally, Kuthayyir praises the beauty of the encounter between Jamīl and Buthayna; in fact, the end of the anecdote suggests that this is a tale oft told by Kuthayyir. Equally important is how the anecdote demonstrates how Jamīl and Buthayna are suitable for each other. Although Kuthayyir may be the poet bearing an encoded message, Buthayna is no stranger to the manipulation of language. To my eyes, Kuthayyir's code is clumsy and obvious; I half expected Buthayna's suspicious father to keep her from the promised tryst or perhaps to set up a trap for Jamīl. Buthayna's diversion signaling her presence and awareness strikes me as far more clever, since she does not address Kuthayyir when she speaks up, but instead instructs her slave girl to help her perform the duty of hospitality. She is a master of the art of misdirection.

Jamīl Buthayna 71

Nor is her choice of meeting place innocent. It might seem odd that Jamīl and Buthayna's encounters are usually at *wādīs*, but, in fact, since women were expected to draw water and do laundry (and men were not), a body of water would be the place least likely to draw the suspicion of any male relatives. If Buthayna wants to steal away from her clan's encampment, it makes sense that she chooses a gender-specific locale and pretext to do so.

Despite its apparent simplicity, the anecdote's language bears closer examination. When Kuthayyir explains to Buthayna's father why he has returned so soon, he says, "Three lines of poetry came to me and I wanted to recite them to you": أن أعرِضها عليك ثلاثةُ أبياتٍ عرَضتُ لي فأحبِبتُ. The verb used to indicate what the three lines of poetry have done and the verb used to indicate what Kuthayyir wants to do with these three lines are in fact the same verb (*'araẓa*), just in different tenses. Of course, Kuthayyir is lying. These three lines of verse do not simply appear, show up, or present themselves. He has manufactured them with an ulterior motive. Kuthayyir, however, *does* simply show up, appear, and present himself. When he speaks to Jamīl Kuthayyir uses a different verb to describe what he intends to do: أنزعِ. *Anza'a*'s meaning here can be guessed from context (a helpful note defines it as reciting poetry), but I've tried to hew as closely as possible to the dictionary definition when translating it as, "I'll toss out a few lines of a poem." Buthayna uses yet another word to describe Kuthayyir's recitation: نشيد *nashīd*, a poem recited in the presence of someone else. The word Kuthayyir uses when he speaks to Jamīl is nonchalant, while the word he uses when he speaks to Buthayna's father implies urgency, and, finally, Buthayna uses a word that insists on her own presence at the recitation. As if this complex relationship between characters and vocabulary were not evidence enough of its sophistication, the anecdote chooses a somewhat uncommon way for Kuthayyir to tell Buthayna's father that he wants to present these supposedly spontaneous lines: أحبِبتُ. This verb is from the same triconsonantal root as *ḥubb*, the most general term for love in Arabic; it is under *ḥubb* that all other words for love are categorized. There are other, more likely ways that Kuthayyir could have expressed a wish to share the verses he pretends have come upon him. By using a verb that contains within it the word for love, again it is as if longing is so contagious that it seeps into language that otherwise has no need to express love. These manipulators of language also seem manipulated *by* language.

72 *Jamīl Buthayna*

Sometimes the language of the anecdote reminds the reader of how the 'Udhrī love poets transformed Arabic poetic language. Although the three lines of poetry ascribed (no doubt erroneously and humorously) to Kuthayyir are truly awful, that does not mean that they serve no literary purpose. The character Kuthayyir's intention to use the first line of recited poetry to grab Buthayna's attention is even more obvious in the Arabic than in the English translation, since no fewer than three of the words share the triconsonantal root *r-s-l*, which is about the sending of a message via a messenger: *irsilu* (is sent), *rasūl* (messenger, i.e. one who bears something sent) and *mursal* (someone to whom something sent is entrusted). Jamīl's encoded message to Buthayna is no more subtle either in its delivery or meaning than are Buthayna's shouts of "Scram!" There is also something perverse about the line from an Islamic perspective, since Muḥammad is *the* messenger bearing God's message. The 'Udhrī poets made love poetry Islamic not by referring to any of the tenets of Islam or by writing devotional poetry, but instead by borrowing from the language of religious devotion to address or speak about the beloved. Kuthayyir is not only a parody of a poet here, but also a parody of a transmitter, since he doesn't transmit Jamīl's poetry but instead just some prosaic, tawdry message. Finally, he is also a messenger *manqué*, falling far short of the Messenger of God in both vehicle (these three lines fall far short of the Qur'ān) and content.

A few pages later another anecdote explores through its very language the complexity of story-telling. The italicized words in bracket are Arabic terms that will be important for the analysis that follows (*KA*, 301–302).

> One day Jamīl was going to visit Buthayna. He dismounted near the water and went in search of one of her slave girls or a shepherdess. His stopping-place was not far from the river bank where an Ethiopian slave-girl was carrying a waterskin. He knew her, since she'd been a go-between for him and Buthayna. She greeted Jamīl and sat with him. He began to talk to her, asking for news of Buthayna, telling her his own news since he'd last parted from Buthayna, and charged her with carrying his message [*risā'ilahu*]. He gave her his signet ring, asking her to hand it over to Buthayna in order to arrange a tryst with her. She agreed and returned to her people, arriving quite late. Buthayna's father, husband and brother were waiting for her and asked her why she was so late. She dissembled, told them nothing

Jamīl Buthayna 73

and made excuses. They gave her a brutal thrashing until she let them know about the situation with Jamīl and handed over the signet ring. Just then two young 'Udhrī men were passing by, overheard the whole matter [*qiṣṣa*] and recognized Jamīl's place in it. Wanting to keep him from harm, they said to the men [*qaum*], "If you come across Jamil while Buthayna is not with him and then you kill him, the evil of the act will adhere to you, even if Buthayna's people are the most powerful of the 'Udhrīs. So give the signet ring back to the slave girl so she can pass it on to Buthayna. When Jamīl visits her you can catch them alone together at night." They said, "You two speak the truth, by my life, so let it be as you suggest." They returned the signet ring to the slave-girl, ordered her to pass it on to Buthayna, and warned her about telling Buthayna that they were aware of the matter [*al-qiṣṣa*]. She did as she was told. Buthayna was unaware of what had happened. The two young men left and went to warn Jamīl. "By God!" he said, "I'm not afraid of them. In my quiver are thirty arrows and not one will miss any of the men among them. And this sword — by God! — I am not one whose hand trembles, nor am I cowardly of heart [*jabān al-janān*]." They beseeched him in the name of God, saying, "Mercy would be better. Stay with us in our tents until the demand [for revenge] abates. Then we will send for her so that she can visit you. Thereafter you can leave safely and beyond reproach." He agreed, saying, "But you must send someone to inform her right now!" So they brought a shepherdess to him and said, "Say what you need." He said, "Go to her and tell her that I wanted to hunt a gazelle, but a band of hunters frightened it off so that it eluded me at night." So she left and informed Buthayna of what Jamīl had said. She was made aware of this matter/his story [*qiṣṣa*], examined it [*baḥatha 'an*] and understood it. As a result, she did not go out to visit him that night. The men kept vigil over her, but as Buthayna did not leave her place, they instead left and followed Jamīl's traces [*yaqtaṣṣuna*]; when they saw the dung of his camel mount they knew he had escaped them.

An episode in the life of a poet whose verse is emblematic of the failure of oral transmission to preserve adequately is recounted in an anecdote in which the transmission and interpretation of narrative is fraught.

In order to lend authority to the words he asks the slave girl to transmit to Buthayna, he hands her his signet ring as evidence to

74 *Jamīl Buthayna*

convince a potentially skeptical Buthayna of their veracity. The transmission of Jamīl's message proves faulty, however, because it is interrupted by Buthayna's most important male relatives: her father, her brother and her husband. What is most interesting here is that while these three men persuade her to reveal Jamīl's *ḥāl* (situation), when two men passing by overhear, this *ḥāl* becomes a *qiṣṣa*. The verb with which *qiṣṣa* shares the same consonantal root, *qaṣṣa*, can mean to pare, to clip or to cut away; or to track someone by following his tracks or footsteps; or either to pursue the course of a story or to tell it or recite it. *Qiṣṣa* then means both the telling of a story and the retracing of this story to its source, *and* the very matter being recounted, with what is not germane to understanding it pared away. This matters because when the two young 'Udhrī men pass by, they witness and overhear not just the beating but interpret the exchange between the slave girl being thrashed and the three men thrashing her and recognize that it leads back to Jamīl. When these two young men address Buthayna's father, brother and husband, these three are not merely three men but form a *qaum*, which in Arabic is one of several words that can be translated "tribe." Related to the verb *qāma*, to stand up, those men who are standing — that is, the men of fighting age — represent the threat of men standing together. The two young men — Arabic has a dual form for nouns, adjectives and verbs — realize that in order to protect their kinsmen Jamīl they must act to prevent the interruption of the transmission of his message to Buthayna by warning Buthayna's husband and kinsmen of the perils of rash action. They propose that the *qaum* stand down and instead of blocking transmission of Jamīl's message they change its outcome. The slave girl will hand over the ring and transmit Jamīl's *qiṣṣa*. It will still be traced back to Jamīl, but the result will not be the reunion of the lovers but instead their separation rendered permanent by Jamīl's justifiable murder made possible by using his *qiṣṣa* to track him down.

The two young 'Udhrī men then proceed to warn Jamīl who at first insists that he will act heroically in his own defense. His heightened, lyrical language (*jabān al-janān*) reminds the reader that he is more poet than warrior (a lover not a fighter). His two kinsmen convince him to remain with them by urging him to be merciful. He insists that a new message be transmitted to Buthayna in coded, even allegorical language. Because there is no physical object to corroborate the veracity of the message this time, it is up to Buthayna to examine it carefully. *Baḥatha 'an*'s literal meaning is to scrape up dust or earth in order to find something. Her act of interpretation (who really sent this to me and what does it mean?) is parallel to the action taken by her father, brother and husband once they realize that Jamīl will not appear. They decide to follow Jamīl's traces; *yaqtaṣṣuna* is formed from the same triconsonantal root as *qiṣṣa*. It means both to track someone and to understand a story. Poor interpreters, the three men are unable to trace the story back to Jamīl. Instead all they end up with is a piece of shit.

Although Buthayna is not as active a participant in this anecdote as in the previous one, Jamīl's survival nonetheless depends on her success as an interpreter. Some thirty pages later, in the final anecdote about Jamīl and Buthayna in the *Book of Songs* her presence barely registers (*KA*, 330):

I'd set out from Taymā' at the last moment of darkness before dawn and saw an old woman on a donkey. She spoke the fine Arabic of a Bedouin. I asked her where she was from. She answered, "I am an 'Udhrī." So I mentioned Jamīl and Buthayna. She said, We were at one of our water-sources in al-Janāb, having deviated from the path because of an army approaching from Syria on its way to Ḥijāz. Our men had gone out on a journey and had left behind a few boys, but they'd gone down early in the evening to a village near us to talk with some of their neighbors, so that there was no one left but Buthayna and I. Suddenly a man came down from the heights to meet us. He greeted us, but we were apprehensive and fearful. I took a good look at him and returned his greeting, for it was Jamīl. I said, "Jamīl?" He replied, "Indeed, by God!" He could barely stay on his feet for hunger, so I went to get one of our bowls in which there was cheese curd and a goatskin with butter and date syrup. I pressed out some of the cheese curd and gave it to him, saying, "Eat this!" so he took it and ate it. I went to get one of our skins in which there had been milk and poured out cold water for him, which he drank, so that his soul returned. I said to him, "You've come to this, encountering such disaster. What's the matter?" He replied, "I was, by God, three days on that flat-topped mountain the two of you see. I watched ceaselessly until I saw an opening. When I saw the young men of your tribe go down to the village, I came straight away to say farewell, for I am heading to Egypt." We spoke for a while and said our farewells, then he departed. He had not been long absent when news of his death reached us.

76 *Jamīl Buthayna*

The anecdote recounts nothing of what Buthayna may have said or done. All the action of the anecdote is accomplished by the narrator remembering her youth, giving food and water to Jamīl (Buthayna does not, e.g. ask her or order her to do so). Nearly all the speech of the anecdote is ascribed to Jamīl. Indeed, the reader would be excused for not noticing Buthayna at all. Is Buthayna's silence and Jamīl's last outburst of volubility poignant? With his death there will be nothing more to tell of her — there is no other poet driven mad by her, nor are there tales of her conjugal life, for obvious reasons. A millennium later bits and pieces of Buthayna as refracted through Jamīl or "Jamīl" or would-be Jamīls will be gathered up and assembled into poems no doubt composed at least in part by glancing details extraneous to the life of this woman from a yet more distant past.

Because the Buthayna poems are so fragmentary, if they are poems at all, in them Buthayna is little more than an inconsistent set of 'Udhrī love poem clichés. The genius of the anecdotes assembled in the *Book of Songs* is found in the portrait of a woman consistently strong-willed and self-aware. She nonetheless depends on Jamīl for an existence beyond the end not of her life but of *his*. Recognition that the anecdote is a vital genre in Arabic Literature (maybe even the preeminent genre, since the Qur'ān is putatively beyond genre) allows the World Lit reader to appreciate the true value of Buthayna and Jamīl, which does not lie in the spurious verse but in the wholly fictional life imagined for them.

Notes

1 "Making Love through Scholarship in Jamīl Buthayna." *The Beloved in Middle East Literatures: The Culture of Love and Languishing.* London: I.B. Tauris, 2017, 156–174.
2 My presentation of these anecdotes does not follow with full accuracy how they appear to the reader of the original Arabic. Each anecdote is preceded by a lengthy retracing of the anecdote's transmission back to its original source: so-and-so reported to so-and-so who reported to so-and-so, etc. This was how an anthologist vouched for the authority of his material. In addition, most of the anecdotes are punctuated by a verse or two of poetry; sometimes the verse or verses interrupt the anecdote. It is likely that the anecdotes were originally invented to explain enigmatic lines of poetry, much as many of the *ḥadīth* (brief narratives about what the Prophet Muḥammad said or did) were probably originally produced to provide narrative context for enigmatic passages of the Qur'ān.

5 Friedrich Rückert's (1788–1866) *Unnachahmlich* Qur'ān

The Qur'ān is beautiful. That might seem like an aesthetic judgment. It might also seem like mere opinion, easily contradicted or disputed. It may also be the sort of bald declaration a scholar should not make. Yet it would be hard to argue that the Qur'ān has not grown more beautiful with the passage of time, that the appreciation of the Qur'ān on aesthetic grounds has not become more widespread, commonplace and institutionalized over the centuries. There has long been something nearly objective about the beauty of the Qur'ān. The way in which this beauty has overflowed the limits of its *sui generis* genre — a recitation transmitted to and among believers — says something about the enduring rigor of belief in its aesthetic qualities. For those who cannot read the Qur'ān, which includes nearly all non-Muslims and a large proportion of Muslims as well, and therefore cannot experience aesthetic pleasure based on either the meaning of the text or how that meaning and its expression are related, there remain two other vital ways to appreciate its beauty. First, a Qur'ān, or a page of the Qur'ān, or even a mere verse of the Qur'ān, written in any one of many styles of calligraphy, may be extraordinarily beautiful, even to someone wholly ignorant of the Arabic script and therefore unable to distinguish letters let alone read words. A non-Muslim non-Arabophone reader can experience the calligraphy of the Qur'ān as beauty in the abstract. The Qur'ān as physical object can be and has been rendered repeatedly into an *objet d'art*. Second, a chapter of the Qur'ān can be recited according to complex rules, which require years of training to master, so that it is rendered extraordinarily pleasing to the ears, as the many Qur'ān recitation competitions across the Muslim world, some of which can be found on YouTube, attest. It is not unusual for a beautiful man with a beautiful, athletic voice to all but sing the Qur'ān to the hushed pleasure of a crowd. The Qur'ān as intangible object can be rendered into a

78   *Friedrich Rückert*

performance that leaves the spectator in a swoon. In neither the case of calligraphy nor the case of professional recitation is the text's meaning of immediate consequence. The Qur'ān as experienced today very nearly marks a perfect cleavage of form from content. The calligraphy is beautiful regardless of the text's meaning, as is the recitation. It is enough to know that the verses written in calligraphy or sung in recitation are from the Qur'ān to predispose the viewer or listener to understand them as beautiful. If any further convincing is still required, the *objet d'art* or the performance accomplishes it.

The Qur'ān is traditionally believed to be untranslatable, stemming from its purported inimitability or إعجاز (*i'jāz*), although this notion postdates the sending-down of the Qur'ān itself by at least two centuries.[1] Like any other literary text dependent on rhythm, rhyme and other qualities particular to the language in which it is written (such as *tajnīs*, or root play, to take just one example from Arabic), the Qur'ān eludes the translator who would attempt to recreate the experience of reading it in the original Arabic for a reader in the target language. The spillover aestheticization of the Qur'ān, which has rendered the text tangible and performative, further complicates the task of the translator, because the Muslim imbued with a knowledge of the work's beauty as represented in calligraphy and professional recitation comes to the text *knowing* (in this case, *connaissance*, as in Claudel) its beauty. The non-Muslim non-Arabophone reader tackling the Qur'ān for the first time in his native language approaches the text stripped of this vital aesthetic context.[2] The experience of the Qur'ān for the believer is necessarily multidisciplinary, which leaves the translator, scholar or teacher, whatever his multidisciplinary bent, woefully inadequate to the task. No doubt the best way to provide the World Lit reader with an adequate experience of the Qur'ān would be to convert him at an early age, or better yet, place the infant pre-reader in a devout, culturally conscious, Arabic-speaking Muslim family. I suspect that few American universities would endorse such a pedagogical strategy.

Those unable or unwilling to be born into a Muslim family or convert at a very early age in order to fully appreciate the Qur'ān's aesthetic resonance must rely on translation (or translations) to convey the text's beauty as best it can. It may be the case that other Semitic languages, such as Hebrew and Amharic, may be the most likely to offer the translator the resources necessary to express the beauty of the text, since they share certain features of Arabic that the Qur'ān exploits to the full, but I am wholly unqualified to read translations in those languages, let alone appreciate them. Unlike a scholar or teacher attempting to convey the qualities of the Qur'ān to his readers or students, the translator must decide, if not from the very beginning, at least fairly early in the process of translation, what form a Qur'ān in English, or Spanish, or French, or Chinese, or Korean will take. The question of what the Qur'ān *is* then becomes unavoidable. Having written an entire book about the relationship of the Qur'ān to poetry (and other genres) that wrung ten years out of my life, I prefer not to belabor the point here. However, it is important to know at the very least that the Qur'ān itself rejects the notion that it is poetry or that Muḥammad was a poet. And, yet, that Qur'ān and poetry have ever since enjoyed, if that's the right word, an intimate relationship in both exegesis and creative expression, is indisputable.

A translator's decision to make poetry of the Qur'ān in order to represent the aesthetic qualities of the text then brings with it an enormous amount of baggage harrowed by the near-endless possibility of intercultural incomprehension. In short, for the purposes of this chapter, it is crucial to remember that what makes nineteenth-century German verse is not what makes seventh-century Arabic verse. The incongruence between the two concepts of poetry and incommensurability of the two practices of poetry — if *Dichtung* and شعر can even be considered the same thing — require the reader to think long and hard about what it means to make a literary text beautiful. Does the discipline of World Literature ask anyone to do that? And if it does, does it also provide the reader with the tools he needs? Is there room in World Literature for scholars and writers grappling in languages other than English with literatures distant from their own?

As if the problem of how to manifest to the unbeliever the beauty of a work of literature sacred to hundreds of millions of people and said to be untranslatable were not complex enough, in this chapter I want to explore *as literature* (rather than as an example of Orientalist scholarship) a nineteenth-century translation of the Qur'ān into German verse. The point of this exploration is not to determine the fidelity of the translation or the suitability of verse to the task, although both these questions are important, but instead imagine ways of presenting the rhetorical beauty of the German text grappling with the Arabic to American readers (who generally do not consider German a beautiful language). Or, perhaps better put, the point is to explore a particular early nineteenth-century German conception of rhetorical beauty

80   *Friedrich Rückert*

transposed from one language to another. Since an American reading the Qur'ān in German might seem an entirely quixotic endeavor, especially because I am writing this while in Hanoi, an analogy may prove useful. Few who have read the King James Bible would dispute that it is a literary work of great beauty, one of the masterpieces of the English language. It is perhaps yet more beautiful than the Hebrew or Greek texts from which it was translated, as the translators created a language for the text so consistent across its many books that a naïve reader might suppose that the entire work was translated from one language rather than two (or three, if the Book of Job is understood to be written in not-quite-Hebrew) and that it all came from one hand.[3] Since, however, it is a translation, how could one possibly teach the King James Bible to a Serbian or Mongolian or Malagasy reader with little or no English? Friedrich Rückert's 1836 translation of the *Qur'ān* into German verse poses a similar quandary for the reader without access to the text through German, with the American reader standing in for the Serbs, Mongols and Malagasy of the previous sentence.

Although I cannot (at least with a straight face) argue that Rückert's verse Qur'ān is as important to German Literature as the King James Bible is to English Literature, Rückert was nonetheless a towering figure during his lifetime, certainly far more famous than any of the individuals who toiled at the translation of the Bible into English in the early seventeenth century. Although another German, Johann Wolfgang von Goethe, has been fetishized by the World Literature crowd for mentioning that he had read a translated Chinese novel, Rückert's translations into German from Arabic, Persian, Turkish, Chinese (via Latin), and numerous other "Oriental" languages make him the single most important source of Asian-language literatures in the history of German culture. Since it would be difficult to over-estimate the German-language contribution to the translation and explication of Asian texts for French-, English-, Russian-, Italian- and Spanish-speaking scholars of Arabic Literature and Islam, Rückert's achievement is then no small feat. Certainly Euro-American understanding of Arabic Literature — indeed, even Arab understanding of Arabic Literature — would be radically different without the scholarship of figures subsequent to Rückert, such as Ignác Goldziher and Theodor Nöldeke of the late nineteenth and early twentieth centuries, and Annemarie Himmel and Angelika Neuwirth of the late twentieth and early twenty-first centuries, just to name a handful. Nonetheless, according to the search function on the kindle app for my laptop, there are no references to Rückert or any of these figures yet 337 references to Goethe in *World Literature in Theory*, a collection of essays edited by David Damrosch (Wiley Blackwell, 2014), or roughly once every page and a half. Seven of the thirty-three contributors mention Goethe's comment about reading this obscure Chinese novel. There are 388 references to Goethe in the *Routledge Companion to World Literature* (2011), again roughly once every page and a half. Five of the fifty contributors mention Goethe's comment about the Chinese novel. Despite its claims to expansion of the canon, World Literature's self-cannibalizing tendency instead encourages shrinkage; the *Welt* of *Weltliteratur* is indeed ever smaller if the *über*-canonical figure Goethe remains its *Prüfstein*.[4]

Although Rückert has never been as internationally renowned as Goethe, he was not only a great scholar and translator, but also an astonishingly productive poet whose verse was anthologized and widely read in the German-speaking world through the beginning of the twentieth century. Unlike Goethe's *Sorrows of Young Werther* or *Faust*, Rückert's more than 10,000 poems are nearly completely forgotten today (Sagarra, 155). A few poems of his may be familiar to aficionados of Gustav Mahler (1860–1911), who set several to music just over a century ago, including five that comprise the *Rückert-Lieder* cycle and another five selected from Rückert's 428 *Kindertotenlieder*, which marked both Rückert and Mahler's coming to terms with the untimely deaths of some of their children. Rückert's disappearance from World Literature as a translator may be even more lamentable than his disappearance from German Literature as a poet, since his Qur'ān was but one among many works of scholarship-translation that set out to make Europeans understand what was at stake in the great works of other literatures. His choices are no less instructive than his intentions and methods. By electing, for example, to translate Abū Tammām's ninth-century *Ḥamāsa*, an anthology of the best lines culled from more than three centuries of Arabic verse by a famous Abbasid poet, he presents German readers with poetry as Arabs themselves had learned it for centuries (in sharp contrast to the work of the famed Italian orientalist, Francesco Gabrieli, who assembled lines of verse into poems that most likely never existed at all, as I demonstrated in Chapter 4) (Weipert, 114). Goethe's offhand remark about a lousy Chinese novel matters less than Rückert's decades constructing translations from the inside of

82 *Friedrich Rückert*

a text out; nonetheless, in these two critical anthologies Goethe scores 725 to Rückert's 0.

Rückert's translation of the Qur'ān was not the first into German — five other translations preceded his — and it is far from the last. It is certainly not the most scholarly, despite the erudition evinced by the care with which he translated it; Rudi Paret's 1966 translation probably qualifies on that count. When evaluating Rückert's achievements, it is important to remember that a nineteenth-century European translator from Arabic had few of the tools available today. Rückert had access to Arabic texts of the Qur'ān that he could borrow from his municipal library and later had his own copy. He had a concordance and books about the life of the Prophet. He even had al-Bayḍāwī's thirteenth-century Qur'ān commentary to consult when he found a verse particularly challenging (al-Bayḍāwī's commentary is better known for its concision than its perspicacity, however). However, Rückert did not have instant access to multiple translations of the Qur'ān, or tome after tome of medieval, Sufi and modern commentaries at his fingertips, as today's scholar-translator might; nor were there yet websites devoted to analyzing the Qur'ān word by word. Rückert had no dictionary of Qur'ānic Arabic, or any sort of dictionary from Arabic to German; such a reference work simply did not yet exist. He relied instead on the seventeenth-century *Lexicon Arabico-Latinum* compiled by Jacob Golius and reworked by Rückert's contemporary Georg Freytag. Despite these impediments, although Rückert's translation of the Qur'ān was incomplete upon his death, it is nonetheless recognized even today as coming closest to reproducing the effect of the original Arabic text on native speakers of Arabic. Annemarie Schimmel goes even further in her praise, insisting "that Rückert's achievement in translation has given the Germans a treasure that no other language possesses" (Schimmel, Kindle location 28).[5] In other words, Rückert's Qur'ān is not simply a great contribution to the study of Arabic Literature and Islam, but is a unique gift to German Literature as well.

Despite Rückert's unrivaled achievement as scholar and translator, it would be a mistake to think that he came out of nowhere, as the desire to reproduce the Qur'ān's beauty predates him. Nonetheless, although Rückert was not the first German scholar to recognize the Qur'ān's aesthetic appeal, and despite this shift in attitude toward Islam and Muḥammad in the late eighteenth and early nineteenth centuries, this was still a minority view (Loop, 457). Some

Friedrich Rückert 83

of Rückert's predecessors and peers also believed that German was the ideal language into which the Qur'ān should be translated. The Viennese Orientalist Josef von Hammer-Purgstall (1774–1856), for example, wrote as early as 1811 in his *Fundgrubens des Orients* (Foundations of the Orient) that

> The highest magic of Arab poetry is not only in image and movement, but also in the rhymes, which are true sirens to Arab ears. Thus, in order to mint the poetic content of the Koran as truly as possible, the translation must not only have the same pace but also the same tone as the original. The final rhymes of the verses must be transmitted as rhymes, which hitherto has not happened in any of the translations known to us, and could not be more faithfully done in any European language than in the German. (Bobzin, xiv)

Hammer-Purgstall well understood the difficulties of the task, having published a few samples of rhymed German translations from the Qur'ān a couple of years prior. Although Rückert seems to have learned from other scholars which aspects of the Qur'ān's rhetoric rendered it powerful, nonetheless he seems to have been the first, perhaps the only, scholar-translator to have at least somewhat successfully moved from recognition to realization.

So what did early nineteenth-century German scholars and translators believe the salient characteristics of the Qur'ān's as literature to be? The orientalist Heinrich Fleischer (1801–1888) spells it out in his review of an 1840 translation by Lion Ulmann (1804–1843):

> The translator of the Qur'ān should neither paraphrase nor explain as such. The oracular tone, the determined brevity, abruptness, and disjointedness, the blurry, ambiguous, dark, and foreboding expression is no less relevant than the sensual freshness and power, the rhetorical splendor and sublimity, to the character of the book.... (Bobzin, xxx–xxxi)

Nearly two centuries later Jan Loop adds that what makes the Qur'ān beautiful to Muslims is its "semantic underdetermination" and "unfathomable semantic depth" (Loop, 461). It is this semantic underdetermination that makes the Qur'ān such an elastic text while its semantic depth enables the near-endless play of its Sufi interpreters (among others), and also makes the text seem curiously

84 *Friedrich Rückert*

high modern, as if it were a long-lost cousin to *Finnegans Wake* or a long poem by Yi Sang (who wrote only short poems). In order to understand the significance of the choices made by Rückert in a few key passages of his translation, I want to consider Hammer-Purgstall's insistence on the importance of end-rhyme (and Rückert's understanding of how rhyme functions in the Qur'ān goes beyond Hammer-Purgstall's), Fleischer's disdain for paraphrase and explanation (which indeed has no place in the Qur'ān; paraphrase, explanation and amplification are relegated to the *hadīth* and commentaries), and Loop's appraisal of the text's productive ambiguity. So how does Rückert reproduce for the German-language reader — and I want to insist on German-language rather than German here, since many in the nineteenth century who read or even wrote scholarship in German were not, strictly speaking, German — the effect of Qur'ānic rhyme and rhythm, the Qur'ān's near-abhorrence of narrative coupled with its stripped-away context, and its polysemy? Is Rückert's Qur'ān sufficiently oracular, disjointed, blurry and foreboding?

All Arabic poetry pre-dating or coterminous with the Qur'ān that has been transmitted is monorhymed; no matter how long the poem is, there is only one end-rhyme. This feature of classical Arabic poetry is so important that some famous poems are known as "the poem that rhymes in x" (al-Shanfarā's *Lāmīyya*, e.g. is "the poem that rhymes in *lām*"). Certainly any translator trying to find 60-odd end-rhymes for one of the pre-Islamic *Mu'allaqāt* in English translation would strain against the rhyme-poverty of the target language. Even in rhyme-rich German monorhyming for 60 lines would be a challenge. The Qur'ān, however, unlike classical Arabic poetry, is not monorhymed and the way the Qur'ān is presented on the page obscures the preponderance of rhyme (although the recitation performances do not do so), so that translators who eschew rhyme when translating the sacred text do not seem to stray as far from the structure of the original as those translators from classical Arabic poetry who avoid rhyme might. If a translator wants to reproduce the way the Qur'ān deploys rhyme, the task is then more complex when translating the Qur'ān than when translating a pre-Islamic poem, since the translation must take into account shifts in the handling of rhyme, shifts that simply do not exist in classical poetry. Since a rhyme scheme is easier to show than to describe, below is an outline of the end-rhymes of *Sūrat al-Raḥmān* (Sūra of the Most Merciful, # 55) in the original Arabic and in Rückert's translation. Rückert divides lines 1–17 somewhat

Friedrich Rückert 85

differently, for reasons I will explain later, but thereafter his verses line up closely with the original Arabic. Throughout the sūra there are also several instances of internal rhyme.

Sūra 55 (Arabic)
verses 1–9 end in -ān
10–11 end in -ām
12–13 end in -ān
14–15 end in -ār
16–23 end in -ān (with one verse ending in ayn)
24 ends in -ām
25–26 end in -ān
27 ends in -ām
28–40 end in -ān
41 ends in ām
42–71 end in -ān (with one verse ending in ūn)
72 ends in -ām
73–77 end in -ān
78 ends in -ām

Sūra 55 (Rückert's German)
1–9 end in -age (with one verse ending in -ache)
10–11 end in -illen/-ülen
12–13 end in -ien
13–16 end in -ennen (with one verse ending in -ehmen)
16–17 end in -gänge
    (verses 1–17 are not broken as they are in the Arabic,
      but 18–78 match perfectly)
18–25 end in -ennen
26–27 end in -ehn
28–30 end in -ennen (with one verse ending in -innen)
30–78 end in -ennen with the following exceptions
    31-innen
    33-innen
    35-önnen
    37-emen
    39-ien
    50-innen
    52-innen
    54-änden
    56-ien
    58-inen

86 Friedrich Rückert

60-önen
62-enen
64-ünen
66-innen
68-ihnen
70-önen
72-ängen
74-enien
76-önen

It is evident that Rückert follows closely the rhyme scheme of the sūra for the first fifteen lines and then the rhyming becomes more approximate, as he tries to keep everything as close to -ennen as possible.[6] Rückert is clearly paying very close attention to shifts in the Arabic text. In order to get some sense of how much it matters that the Arabic end-rhymes shift from -ān to -ām to -ār, I listened to three different recitations of this sūra. This, of course, raises the question of *which* Qur'ān is being translated, since the recitations uploaded to YouTube are all recent and therefore the end-product of nearly a millennium and a half of an art form that has no doubt evolved significantly. I would nonetheless speculate that the variation in rhyme in the Arabic original is meaningful in two ways. First, this distinguishes the Qur'ān from poetry of the time, as I've already mentioned. Since Rückert also translated a great deal of Arabic poetry, he was aware of this. Second, the irregularity of the rhyme draws attention to other musical qualities of the text, especially its rhythm, which is based on patterns of long and short vowels. Since German poetry is built upon units of stressed and unstressed syllables (as is English) rather than on a pattern of alternating long and short vowels, it would be very difficult to mimic this aspect of Arabic verse. Hammer-Purgstall and Rückert's emphasis on getting the rhymes right stems at least in part from the relative ease with which German can mimic that aspect of Arabic poetry in contrast to other aspects.

Since Sūra 55 concerns itself with God's gift of eloquence to humanity, it may then be a particularly appropriate section of the Qur'ān to analyze for an understanding of how Qur'ānic rhetoric functions. The first twelve lines mention God's many gifts to humanity in a sort of recapitulation of Creation. The ensuing sixty-six lines switch to lines alternating between either the mention of one of these gifts of Creation *or* a form of punishment to be visited on the unbeliever with a sort of refrain in the form of a repeated question (the only such refrain in the Qur'ān): فَبِأَيِّ ءَالَاءِ رَبِّكُمَا تُكَذِّبَانِ؟

Friedrich Rückert 87

For obvious reasons, understanding a question posed thirty times over seventy-eight lines is crucial to understanding the overarching meaning and aesthetic appeal of the sūra itself. There are two complications any translator must face in rendering this question into German or English. The first is that the question is in the dual grammatical form, which exists in neither English nor German, meaning here that it is addressed to two people. The obvious solution would be to refer to the addressees as "you two" or "you both" or "ihr beide," although in English it sounds odd when said thirty times in succession.[7] It must have seemed awkward in German as well, for Rückert finds a way around it. I offer first the Arabic, then my clunky and literal translation from the Arabic intended to show where the difficulties lie, then Rückert's German, then my equally and clunky and literal translation from the German (Rückert, 398):

١٣ فَبِأَيِّ ءَالَاءِ رَبِّكُمَا تُكَذِّبَانِ؟

13. And which of the bounties of your (dual) Lord would you (dual) reject as a lie?

12–13. Ihr Menschen und Ihr Genien!
 Welch Gnad' eures Herrn wollt ihr verkennen?

12–13. You (plural) Men and you (plural) Jinn!
Which of your (plural) Lord's favors do you (plural) misjudge?

Rather than repeat "ihr beide" or something similar thirty times, Rückert inserts a line that is found nowhere in the Arabic, making clear who is being addressed in the question that immediately follows: man and jinn. Bobzin's note to Rückert's text speculates that he does this in order to insert yet another end-rhyme, but since there are already so many of them in the translation, this explanation makes little sense (Rückert, 548). Instead Rückert wants to dualize as best as he can in German his non-dual rendering and thereby avoid the awkwardness of phrasing ("ihr beide" thirty times) that would irritate the German ear through repetition.

So here Rückert's German Qur'ān diverges from the Arabic. The addition of this line tempers the text's vaunted abruptness and smooths out its admirable disjointedness, thereby diverging from the rhetorical characteristics ascribed to the Qur'ān by his predecessors and contemporaries. Here Rückert's translation strategy allows the German-language reader to understand the complexity of the "you" in the question-refrain, while the Arabic reader must wait until after the question is first posed and then extrapolate the identity of the

88 *Friedrich Rückert*

dual you from a certain duality of creation found in verses 14 and 15. The Arabic, followed by my literal translation, reads:

خَلَقَ ٱلإنسَانَ مِن صَلْصَالٍ كَٱلْفَخَّارِ ١٤
وَخَلَقَ ٱلْجَانَّ مِن مَّارِجٍ مِن نَّارٍ ١٥

14. He created Mankind from clay, like pottery,
15. While he created Jinn from a smokeless flame of fire.

Rückert offers (Rückert, 398):

14. Er schuf den Menschen Töpfergleich aus Lehmen,
15. Und schuf die Genien aus des Funkens Brennen;
14. He created Mankind potter-like out of clay,
15. And created Jinn out of the spark burning.

The Qur'ān then addresses both Mankind and the Jinn for the rest of the sūra, implying that both share in God's favor and potential disfavor. Rückert's translation, it seems to me, captures the spirit of these two lines while also hewing closely to its form. And while he chooses not to introduce some German equivalent of the dual-form he nonetheless finds a way to suggest the duality of the plural form of you he uses instead.

The second complication in translating the question-refrain is the verb *kadhdhaba*, which occurs in one form or another 176 times in the Qur'ān. It is often translated as "to deny" or "to reject," but here the denying or rejecting stems from disbelief, as *kadhdhaba* is related to *kidhb* (a lie) and *kadhūb* (liar). Rückert's choice, *verkennen*, means a failure to recognize something for what it is, while the addition of the modal verb *wollen* (wollt) implies a certain willful failure to recognize the truth of God's bounty. Beginning here the sūra falls into a sort of call-and-response pattern. Clearly my overly literal and punctilious translation would never make it past an editor if I intended it as part of a complete text intended for the general reader. Rückert manages to suggest the meaning of the line without explaining or paraphrasing. Its only weakness is that it fails to indicate that the address is dual, although, as I've pointed out above, he manages to indicate the duality of the plural *ihr* another way. Nonetheless when this duality spills over into the next few lines, with references to *mashriqayn, maghribayn*, and *baḥrayn*, all in the dual form, it comes as even more of a surprise in the German translation because the reader is unprepared. Rückert's "beiden Sonnaufgänge,"[8] "beiden Niedergänge" and "beiden Wasser" (both sunrises, both sunsets, and both bodies of water) therefore feel somewhat unmoored. Returning to the Arabic, the *mashriq* is the place where the sun rises (or the east — "Morgenland" would not be the worst German translation), while the *maghrib* is the place where the sun sets (or the west — "Abendland" would do as well as "Morgenland"). The Arabic insists that there are places where the sun rises and two places where the sun sets, while *baḥrayn* means "two seas." There is no immediately obvious reason for this doubling-up of east, west or sea. As a result, the traditional explanations tend to be complex, unconvincing and hoary. As far as I can tell from study aids and web pages devoted to explicating the Qur'ān, these two wests and two easts are understood as references to the divergence of the summer and winter solstices (Nasr, Kindle location 63282). This understanding dates back to at least the ninth century, as al-Ṭabarī's commentary indicates. And yet this verse's semantic underdetermination is sufficient to allow a radically different Sufi interpretation also from the ninth century; for example, al-Tustarī's commentary understands the rising and setting to be of the heart and the tongue, which rise through sincerity and set in indication of subservience (www.altafsir.com). I suspect that it may simply be the case that the pleasure of introducing the dual form leads the Qur'ān to start placing nouns in the dual form as well. In any case, true to Fleischer's assertion that the Qur'ān is ambiguous and disjointed — powerfully so — the duality of these terms remains unexplained and therefore open to interpretation in Rückert's translation, just as they are in the original Arabic, despite the near-unanimity of the commentaries (even al-Tustarī's Sufi commentary acknowledges the summer and winter solstice explanation before offering its own interpretation). Bobzin's note in the appendix giving the standard explanation for the mysteriously doubled east and west strikes me as a disservice to Rückert's translation, which goes to great lengths to maintain semantic depth. The note is a prosaic termination of interpretation, which Rückert's lyrical translation works hard to prevent.

Does Rückert's translation sound like the Arabic? The correct answer can only be: no, of course not. As the two languages do not sound much alike, the original and the translation cannot sound much alike. Nonetheless, a comparison of the question-refrain in transliterated Arabic (so that the reader untrained in the Arabic alphabet can follow along) and in the German translation may indicate a shift in emphasis in the German translation. This shift, however, actually works to align the message of the translation with that of the original. The bars above the vowels in the transliteration

90 *Friedrich Rückert*

indicate long vowels; un-barred vowels are short. The distinction between short and long vowels is used to great effect in Qur'ān recitations, highlighting the text's musicality.

> *fa bi'ayyi 'ālā'i rabbikumā tukadhdhibāni*
> Welch Gnad' eures Herrn wollt ihr verkennen?

In both the Arabic and the German, the final and rhyming word of the question-refrain is the verb indicating the action of the addressees. Putting the word in this position, natural in German with its penchant for putting verbs at the end of sentences, is not where one would put the verb in everyday Arabic speech, but since Qur'ānic Arabic is inflected (like Latin and Russian), word order is more malleable than in most Western European languages. Listening to recitations made me realize that the use of the dual serves to further emphasize the act of negation and disbelief represented by *tukadhdhibāni*. The long *ā* in the penultimate syllable is drawn out when recited. Both men and jinn do the same thing over and over and over; while God's creation is various and multiple. The question is short, in both the Arabic and the German, with most of the verses about God's creation or his punishments longer and more complex. The dual form lengthens words in Arabic, emphasizing the responsibility of these two groups of creatures. In like fashion, the only three-syllable word in the German question is *verkennen*, representing the mistaken and dangerous actions of men and jinn. All the other words are one syllable long (*welch* and *gnad* are shortened versions of *welche* and *Gnade*), except *eures*, but which is so common that it barely registers as two syllables. Again, although Rückert did not find an easy way to translate the dual form, it is evident that his translation attempts with great precision to reproduce the effects of the Arabic original in the German.

What I find most refreshing about Rückert and his like-minded predecessors and contemporaries is their desire to understand the Qur'ān and how it works on its own terms. Unlike Goethe, for whom what is interesting about the famous-yet-obscure Chinese novel, whichever one it might have been, is not anything in the novel but instead that it is Chinese, for Rückert the Qur'ān is interesting for how it is meaningful within the constraints imposed by its language and exigencies of its form. This is what Rückert wants to reproduce; if to his reader this German Qur'ān is strange, he wants it to be strange as the Qur'ān in Arabic is strange to *its* reader, rather than strange merely because it was written down by

Friedrich Rückert 91

Arabs. There is a tendency (although it is by no means universal) among those in the World Literature crowd to reproduce Goethe's attitude toward the Chinese novel; what is interesting for most of them is *not* the Chinese novel (what's in it, how it is written, how does it work) but that Goethe read a Chinese novel at all. It is indeed interesting that Goethe read a Chinese novel, but in the end not very interesting, for after all the text is absent, much as the Chinese text is absent from Claudel and many texts are absent from World Literature (Chapter 2). What would have been interesting is some sort of sustained engagement on Goethe's part with what the novel meant or even was. Otherwise World Literature is nothing more than checking boxes.

Notes

1 The scholarship on *i'jāz* is vast. Although G.E. Von Grunebaum's *Encyclopaedia of Islam* article on the topic is marred by its obsessive comparison to biblical aesthetics, it nonetheless points out the key texts of Islamic thinkers from the ninth century. A.H. Johns names Ibn Qutayba as the earliest scholar (d. 889) of the discipline of *i'jāz* (Von Grunebaum, 1018–1020; Johns, 81).

2 In *What is Islam? The Importance of Being Islamic* (Princeton, 2016), his tour-de-force book-length essay that sets out to convince the thoughtful twenty-first-century Euro-American reader to imagine a different way of understanding Islam, Shahab Ahmed not only reinserts Islam into its wider cultural context, but makes this very context what he means by "Islam." Wahhābī Islam, propagated throughout the Muslim world with petrodollars, and what most non-Muslim Euro-Americans have come to think of as Islam, means to strip Islam of most of this context (just as it has stripped Mecca of nearly every vestige of its history) and thereby, if we push Ahmed's argument to its logical conclusion, de-Islamifies itself.

3 I read neither Hebrew nor Greek, so cannot comment on the aesthetic qualities of the texts behind the King James Bible. However, Robert Alter's many translations from the Hebrew Bible, as well as his works such as *The Art of Biblical Poetry* (1985) easily convince the non-specialist of its complexity and artistry. I am unaware of any scholars championing the beauty of the Greek of the New Testament.

4 B. Venkat Mani's "Bibliomigrancy. Book series and the making of world literature" and Jing Tsu's "World Literature and National Literature(s)" are two brilliant contributions to the Routledge *Companion* that explore the complexity of the account of Goethe's ephemeral intersection with Chinese Literature.

5 In 2009 Jan Loop, a historian of the European reception and translation of the Qur'ān, writes of "Friedrich Rückert's unsurpassed poetical translation of the Koran" (Loop, 457). Taha Badri adds that "it is still the only German translation that conveys the sensual power and

92 *Friedrich Rückert*

linguistic beauty of the Koran" (Badri, 47). Nor is his Qur'ān alone worthy of praise: "Later Persian scholars have confirmed that reading Rückert's 'Oriental' verse is like reading their native poets in translation" (Sagarra, 166).

6 Rückert's careful attention to rhyme is underlined by a comparison of two versions of Sūra 91. Not only are the rhymes entirely different; but Rückert shifts from monorhyme to two sets of close rhyme. The move from one set of close rhymes to another follows a change in topic within the sūra.

7 A.J. Arberry, who penned the best-known scholarly translation in English, uses the unfelicitous "you and you." The popular Ahmadiyya translation into German chooses "ihr beide." Rudi Paret translates "ihr (Dual, auch im folgenden)" (you [plural, also in what follows]) (Paret, 377).

8 "Sonnaufgänge" seems to be a variant on "Sonnenaufgänge." I have not found it anywhere other than in Rückert's translation of the Qur'ān.

6 Yi Ok (1760–1815)

Man out of Time

李鈺 이옥 Yi Ok[1] is not a household name in Korea and is all but absent from World Literature, only a few lines of his poetry having been translated from the original into English, to the best of my knowledge, and a selection of his prose into German in 2010.[2] His work has, however, been translated into Korean; or, at least, paraphrased in Korean. It might seem odd that a Korean writer requires translation into Korean, but, in fact, a great many Korean writers require such translation. Until the end of the nineteenth century most Korean poetry was written using Chinese characters, although centuries earlier King Sejong the Great (1397–1450) had brought about the invention of a native Korean script (he may even have devised it himself). The 兩班 양반 *yangban* literati class[3] was resistant to this new script (today called 한글 *hangeul*, which means "great script," but is also a homonym for "Korean script"), because the years of training required for proficiency in reading and writing Chinese characters restricted literacy and therefore access to knowledge and through it power. Only in 1894 was *hangeul* mandated for official state documents (Sohn, 29). One of the ironies of this resistance to *hangeul*, which is today celebrated in Korea as a brilliant indigenous invention, right up there with kimchi (every provincial or municipal museum of Korean culture devotes a great deal of space to both), is that few Koreans today can read the classics of Korean Literature in the original. That Yi Ok must be paraphrased for the non-specialist Korean reader is therefore not as strange as it might at first seem.

So if few Koreans can read him and even fewer have read him, then why should we (whoever we might be) read Yi Ok? I am not going to argue that his poetry is so terrible that we should read it. Nor am I going to argue that Euro-American scholars have misplaced him through misjudgment of the value of the genre he writes; Euro-American scholars haven't acknowledged his existence, which

94 Yi Ok

puts him beyond the reach of misjudgment and misunderstanding. I cannot recycle any of the other arguments I've made in the first five chapters of this book either. Instead I will argue that Yi Ok merits a place in World Literature because there is nowhere else for him to go. His work only makes sense when considered from a perspective beyond the limits of one national literature. A very well-educated Chinese reader could puzzle through much of his work, but a great deal would make little sense because of the many references to Korean culture. A very well-educated Korean reader could puzzle through the work with access to a heavily annotated paraphrase, but even the paraphrases often resort to simple transliteration of the Korean pronunciation of Chinese characters with little attempt to explain them. If a North American reader had access to a translation (none exists) in an anthology (it isn't there), with hyperlinks and illustrations and notes and transliterations (there aren't any) so that he could also *hear* the poem, he could puzzle through it insofar as scholars and pedagogues would make it possible. Since Yi Ok cannot then be read by anyone, I would argue that simply being beyond reach makes him a valuable addition to World Literature. Although there are points of intersection between Yi Ok and what we know (he is ironic and we like irony; he is heroic and we need heroism; he is complex and the world is no simple place), in the end we do not understand; and we need to understand that we do not understand.

Perhaps Yi Ok's strangest and most compelling work is his 俚諺 이언 *Yi Oen Vulgar Maxims*.[4] It is unlike any other work of Korean Literature that I have read or read about, and yet it is somehow also quintessentially Korean. It is a poem of 264 lines divided into four sections of unequal length. The work as a whole is preceded by three prefaces, titled 一難 일난 *Il Nan The First Difficulty*, 二難 이난 *Yi Nan The Second Difficulty*, and 三難 삼난 *Sam Nan The Third Difficulty*, in which Yi Ok replies to questions from a somewhat clueless but amiable and likely fictive interlocutor. The four sections of the poem are 雅調 아조 *A Cho Song of Refinement*, 艶調 염조 *Yoem Cho Song of Splendor*, 宕調 탕조 *Tang Cho Song of Dissipation* and 悱調 비조 *Bi Cho Song of Inexpression*. Preceding each of these individual sections is a brief description offering an explanation of its title and guidance on how it is to be read. Each of the four sections is spoken in the voice of a woman, or at the very least from the perspective of a woman. They reflect on the experiences of women ranging from betrothal to the aftermath of the death of one's husband. Oddly, there is very little about children in this poem; the subject comes up only in the form of every family's desire for children and the inability to bear children. In other words, the women of this poem are fiancées, wives, courtesans, daughters, daughters-in-law and widows, but never mothers. It is hard to imagine that this elision is accidental; Yi Ok wants to focus on how women are defined in relation to men within and beyond marriage, which he explains in the second preface (*The Second Difficulty*) (Yi, 4, 277):

夫天地萬物之觀, 莫大於觀於人; 人之觀, 莫妙乎觀於情; 情之觀, 莫眞乎觀乎男女之情.

In the examination of the ten thousand things of heaven and earth, nothing is greater than the examination of mankind; in the examination of mankind, nothing is more profound than the examination of emotion; in the examination of emotion, nothing is more true than the examination of emotion between men and women.

Yi Ok seems to suggest a nearly scientific purpose to his exploration of relations between men and women. I suspect that adding children and motherhood would have risked injecting a sort of sentimentality that is wholly absent from the poem. The problem with this summary and with summaries in general, I suppose, is that it smooths away all that is odd about Yi Ok's *Yi Oen*. Much of the rest of this chapter will compensate by emphasizing what is odd about it.

Before speculating as to why Yi Ok chose to write *Vulgar Maxims*, I should explain how I came across his work, not because I am eager to wax autobiographical, but because how I discovered *Vulgar Maxims* may help demonstrate why the poem is so unusual and yet so obviously necessary. It is certainly not the first text one expects a newcomer to the study of Korean Literature to take up. While reading widely about eighteenth-century Chinese women poets (see Chapter 1), I came across a reference to a Korean diplomat interested in purchasing the calligraphy produced by a Chinese woman poet in Changzhou, China, in the early nineteenth century (Mann, 2007, 90). As a result, I thought that I might better understand the phenomenon of eighteenth-century Chinese women poets if I learned something about their counterparts in Korea. Upon further investigation, I was astonished to discover that there were no women poets in eighteenth-century Korea. I have since learned that this is not exactly true, but a few statistics demonstrate how

96   *Yi Ok*

close to true it is. "Of more than 4,000 surviving classical shijo poems [written in *hangeul*], only 92 can be ascribed to women on the basis of diction and content, and of these only 59 are attributable to known women authors," and, as far as I have been able to determine, none of these 59 are from the eighteenth century (Kim, 1996, 111). The great age of Korean women's poetry seems to have been the sixteenth century, and mostly on the basis of a handful poems ascribed to one woman poet, about whom more later. Out of ignorance I had assumed that certain aspects of cultural development would have followed along similar trajectories in China and Korea — and to some degree this is true. However, China and Korea have radically different literary histories, in part, oddly, because Korea borrowed so heavily from China, importing 60% of its vocabulary from Chinese, along with Confucianism and its attendant exam system.

Instead of poetry by Korean women I found poetry in the voice of Korean women as ventriloquized by Yi Ok. Since Korean women were not speaking for themselves, I would have to make do with Yi Ok speaking for them. Of course, it is not true that Korean women were not speaking for themselves; they were merely speaking for themselves in a way that was almost entirely inaudible to men. For example, roughly 6,000 歌詞 (sometimes 歌辭) 가사 *gasa*, another genre of poetry written in *hangeul*, composed by women have reached us from the second half of Joseon in manuscript form. This might sound like a lot, especially in comparison to the statistics for *shijo*, but the extant works of merely one male poet from the same period sometimes exceed 2,000 (Haüßler, 143). Those *gasa* composed by women circulated primarily within her extended family. Over the course of eighteenth-century Korea's ever-more stringent adoption of Confucian mores, which insisted on keeping men and women separate and moving women into their husbands' families (heretofore husbands had moved into their brides' families' households), likely incited the development of the female *gasa*, since once removed from their own families women could only communicate through writing with mothers, sisters and cousins. Since these poems were unpublished, it may be that Yi Ok knew nothing about them. He certainly gives no indication of any familiarity with them.[5]

I remain somewhat puzzled by Yi Ok's near-absence from Korean historical consciousness. Koreans are fascinated by their own history. Or, I should say, popular culture makes much of

Korea's often melodramatic history. The parade of novels, films and TV mini-series that recreate, to one degree or another of historical (in)accuracy, the lives of Koreans in the ever-receding past is astonishing. As of June 2017, six of the ten highest-grossing Korean films ever are historical dramas (https://en.wikipedia.org/wiki/List_of_highest-grossing_films_in_South_Korea). Neither the difficulty of Yi Ok's poetry nor the paucity of details about his life should then be a barrier to his popularization. Precious little is known of the poet 黃眞伊 황지니 Hwang Jini's life — and what is known is legendary — but that did not prevent the success of an eponymous mini-series that ran in 2006. The show had little to do with poetry and a great deal to do with Hwang Jini's career as a sixteenth-century *gisaeng* (a sort of courtesan, skilled in conversation and the arts, trained to keep the *yangban* company). Another poet honored with his own TV show is 丁若鏞 정약용 Jeong Yakyong (1762–1836), who is tricked out as a Korean Sherlock Holmes complete with magnifying glass in *Korean Mystery Detective Jeong Yakyong*, which aired 2009–2010. It is a silly mystery-of-the-week series filled with intentionally amusing anachronisms and engages not at all with Jeong Yakyong's poetry. In any case, Jeong Yakyong is remembered primarily not as a poet but as a philosopher and reformer whose extended family was decimated by the anti-Catholic persecutions of the early nineteenth century, while Hwang Jini is recalled not so much as a poet, but instead as the beautiful and talented *gisaeng* who outwits men. Yi Ok, too, has an interesting, if slim, biography that would not only do well as the source for a Korean historical drama, but also illuminates the constraints of literary life in eighteenth-century Korea, constraints that are crucial to an understanding of *Yi Oen*.

Yi Ok was born into a poor noble family.[6] His only chance for success was to pass a series of exams, modeled on those of the Chinese, in order to demonstrate his mastery of the neo-Confucian canon required for appointment to a government post. In 1792 King Jeongjo (1752–1800) personally read Yi Ok's examination essay, found it written in an inappropriately casual style, and sentenced him to an internal exile that would last nine years. Furthermore, even after King Jeongjo ended his exile, he still would not permit Yi Ok to sit for another examination, thereby ending all hope of an official career. Accusing (and convicting all at once) the poet of writing in an inappropriately casual style meant that the king believed that his examination essay did not hew closely to the rules governing expression in

98   Yi Ok

文言 (Chinese *wenyan*), the concise, elegant literary and administrative language of China and Chinese-influenced cultures, which the Koreans call 漢文 (한문 *hanmun*, literally "Chinese writing"). King Jeongjo expected Yi Ok, and indeed all examinees, to write in the style of the great Confucian classics, which the scholars had not only studied but also memorized. As I will demonstrate, the depth of Yi Ok's immersion into the Confucian classics means that any deviation from their style is also circumscribed by their example. When Yi Ok justifies certain aspects of his poetry, he does so with recourse to the very texts that have been used to justify the limits against which he strains. Yi Ok is nothing if not consistent in his paradoxes and contradictions. Yi Ok's exclusion from any sort of government position would seem to have enabled empathy for others — such as women — who were also excluded from access to power. I do not want to read Yi Ok allegorically, for the poem feels too messy for the one-to-one correspondences demanded by true allegory, but it is difficult not to imagine his own suspended career as the source of Yi Ok's sympathetic portrayal of women unable to control their destinies.

There is much that is strange about *Yi Oen*, but perhaps what is most strange is that the tools Yi Ok has mastered are wholly inappropriate for the task he sets for himself. Written language was gendered in Choseon Korea, with *hanmun* (Chinese writing) reserved almost exclusively for men, and *hangeul* (Korean), which although not reserved for the use of women, was the only means of writing that all but a vanishingly small number of Korean women had at their disposal. Yet Chinese characters are not only an unwieldy tool for representing Korean speech, which has very little in common with Chinese, but this sort of concise and restrained prose was not intended to represent the quotidian thoughts and experiences that Yi Ok intended to capture in his poem, whether in Korean, any Chinese language, Vietnamese or Japanese. It is not a language of everyday communication. Despite his failed exam essay, that Yi Ok had mastered *hanmun* is certain. That Yi Ok also recognizes that his mastery of *hanmun* is a problem is clear from the beginning of his first preface (*The First Difficulty*). He is asked about the suitability of the title, *Yi Oen* (*Vulgar Maxims*) with other more appropriate titles suggested. Classical Chinese prose — certainly this example of Classical Chinese prose — is difficult to translate into either Korean or English, so I will paraphrase and explain rather than translate, especially since Yi Ok insists on ambiguity (Yi, 4, 273–274).

或問曰: "子之俚諺, 何爲而作也? 子何不爲國風爲樂府爲詞曲, 而必爲是俚諺也歟?"

余對 曰: "是非我也, 有主而使之者. 吾安得爲國風樂府詞曲, 而不爲我俚諺也哉? 觀乎國風之爲 國風, 樂府之爲樂府, 詞曲之不爲國風樂府, 而爲詞曲也, 則我之爲俚諺也, 亦可知矣." 曰: "然則, 彼國風與樂府與詞曲, 與子之所謂俚諺者, 皆非作之者之所作歟?" 曰: "作之者, 安敢作也? 所以爲作之者之所作者, 作之矣. 是誰也? 天地萬物, 是已也. 天地 萬物, 有天地萬物之性, 有天地萬物之象, 有天地萬物之色, 有天地萬物之聲."

Someone asked, "As for your *Vulgar Maxims*, why do you call it this and make it this way? Shouldn't you call it something like *Airs of the States* or *Music Bureau Poems* or even *ci* poems or *qu* poems, rather than *Vulgar Maxims*?"

I replied, "This isn't up to me, there are fundamentals one must apply. Why should I call it *Airs of the States* or *Music Bureau Songs* or *ci* or *qu*, and not *Vulgar Maxims*? Seeing as the *Airs of the States* are called *Airs of the States* and *Music Bureau Songs* are called *Music Bureau Songs,* while the *ci* and *qu* are not called *Airs of the States* or *Music Bureau Songs*, but instead are called *ci* and *qu*, so mine is called *Vulgar Maxims,* for obvious reasons."

He said, "In that case, these *Airs of the State* and *Music Bureau Songs* and *ci* and *qu*, as well as what you call *Vulgar Maxims*, were they not all made by their makers?"

I replied, "Make? How does one dare make? The maker of that which has been made, who would that be? The ten thousand things of Heaven and Earth, that's who. The ten thousand things of Heaven and Earth contain the essence of the ten thousand things of Heaven and Earth, the image of the ten thousand things of Heaven and Earth, the color of the ten thousand things of Heaven and Earth, and the sound of the ten thousand things of Heaven and Earth."

Yi Ok bulldozes over his interlocutor with dazzling rhetoric and metaphysical logic that does not address the question. One sentence reads more like a tongue twister than an argument (I offer it in Chinese characters, transliterated according to modern standard Chinese pronunciation, in *hangeul* and transliterated according to modern Korean pronunciation):

100   *Yi Ok*

作之者, 安敢作也? 所以爲作之者之所作者, 作之矣. 是誰也?
zuòzhīzhě āngǎnzuòyě suǒyǐwéizuòzhīzhězhīsuǒzhě zuòzhīyǐ
   shìhéiyě
작지자 안감작야 소이위작지자지소작자 작지의 시수야
chakchicha   ankamchakya   so'i'ouichakchichachisochakcha
   chakchi'ouei sisuya
Make? How does one dare make? The maker of that which has
been made, who would that be?

The rhetorical pyrotechnics of the prefaces differ substantially
from the language of the poetry itself. Yi Ok goes all out *hanmun*
on his reader. The content of the exchange merits some explanation.

Yi Ok's interlocutor is puzzled by the title the poet has chosen for
this work. He considers it entirely inappropriate for a poem composed in *hanmun*. He suggests various other titles: *Airs of the States*
refers to a section of *The Classic of Poetry*, a key text some 2,500
years old appropriated by Confucian commentators by the Han
dynasty. *The Music Bureau* refers to a Han dynasty office responsible for gathering poetry and later becomes the name of a genre
of Chinese poetry. The *ci* is the premier lyric genre of the Song dynasty, while the *qu* is the premier lyric genre of the Yuan dynasty.
In other words, the man says, you are writing in Chinese and have
numerous genres of Chinese poetry from which to choose the genre
of your own poem. And, of course, these genres of Chinese poetry
are familiar to his readers, all of whom are steeped in Chinese Literature, otherwise they would be unable to read *Yi Oen*. One of
the reasons the title *Yi Oen* might be considered inappropriate is
that the adjective *oen* was also used to describe the Korean writing
system before the term *hangeul* was invented: 漢文 한문 *hanmun*
was Chinese writing while 諺文 언문 *oenmun* was vulgar writing.
To further confuse things, most editions of *Yi Oen* do not give the
original Chinese characters of the three prefaces, but instead provide Korean paraphrases only. This gives the mistaken impression
that Yi Ok writes in *hangeul* to explain why he writes in *hanmun*.
Despite having composed the poem and the prefaces in *hanmun*, Yi
Ok refuses to categorize his *Yi Oen* with other Chinese texts.

Despite this refusal, Yi Ok nonetheless has no compunction about
then contradicting himself and arguing his case from the Chinese
classics. In the second preface (*The Second Difficulty*), his interlocutor
asks Yi Ok why he spends so much time on 粉脂裙釵之事 (matters related to powder, rouge, skirts and hairpins), reducing women to their
accessories. He invokes the example of the ancients, citing Confucius

非禮勿聽, 非禮勿視, 非禮勿言 (hear nothing improper, see nothing improper, say nothing improper). Not to be out-cited, Yi Ok says that Confucius is the perfect model for *Vulgar Maxims*, since so many of the poems in the *Classic of Poetry* are spoken by women. Driving his point home, he asks 誰取之? (Who collected them?). The answer: 孔子也 (Confucius did). 誰註之? (Who annotated them?) 集註朱子也, 箋註漢儒也 (Zhu Xi (1130–1200)) gathered the annotations that had been put to paper by Confucian scholars of the Han). This trifecta of authority is unassailable, the greatest neo-Confucian scholar Zhu Xi (whose influence over Confucianism is probably greater than that of Confucius himself), the Han scholars who painstakingly wrote down the Confucian commentaries that had been scattered if not destroyed by Emperor Qin (259–210 BCE) when he attempted to squelch Confucianism, and Confucius himself. Yi Ok is adamant that *Vulgar Maxims* is something other than a retread of the Chinese classics, despite having been written in *hanmun*, and yet he also insists that its subject matter is validated by three pillars of Confucianism.

The interlocutor does have a point when he asks Yi Ok about the powder, rouge, skirts and hairpins. The poem is obsessed with the accoutrements of women. So obsessive, in fact, that one Korean scholar has written an article reconstructing late Joseon dress based on the details given in the poem, because "it includes detailed and various descriptions of everyday clothing worn by strict noblemen, which is difficult to find elsewhere" (Choi, 18). The function of clothing, make-up and accessories differs from one section of the poem to another; indeed, the relationship of the four different women to forms of adornment serves as a vehicle for the message of each section. With the exception of the bride in the first section of the poem, all the women appear to be illiterate or at least completely unconcerned with reading and writing (the first alludes to her knowledge of *hangeul*, referring to it as vulgar writing, in stanza 6). Clothing, make-up and accessories such as hairpins seem to replace writing as a form of expression. Indeed, just as Yi Ok's interlocutor in the three prefaces uses 粉脂裙釵 (powder, rouge, skirts and hairpins) as shorthand for women, the only physical description we get of the women is of what they wear or what they apply to their faces.

The young bride in Section 1 雅調 아조 *A Jo Song of Refinement* spends much of her time embroidering and making clothes for her new husband. Yi Ok explains at the beginning that the *Song of Refinement* relates the young woman's 愛敬勤儉 "love, respect, diligence and thriftiness." Stanzas 8–14 interweave her hard work on behalf of her husband with two references to her own adornment (Yi: 4, 284).

102　*Yi Ok*

8.
養蠶大如掌
下階摘柔桑
非無東海紬
要驗趣味長

9.
爲郎縫衲衣
花氣惱儂倦
回針搯襟前
坐讀淑香傳

10.
阿姑賜禮物
一雙玉童子
未敢顯言佩
結在流蘇裏

11.
小婢牕隙來
細喚阿哥氏
思家如不禁
明日送轎子

12.
艸綠相思緞
雙針作耳囊
親結三層蝶
倩手奉阿郎

13.
人皆戲鞦韆
儂獨不與偕
宣言臂力脆
恐墜玉龍釵

14.
包以日紋褓
貯之皮竹箱
手剪阿郎衣
手香衣亦香

8

I raise silkworms big as the palm of my hand;
I go down the steps to pick soft mulberry leaves.
It doesn't matter that it isn't Eastern Sea silk;
What's essential is taking interest in their growth.

9

I make and mend clothes for my husband
Until the scent of flowers wears me out.
I return the needle to its place in front of a shirt collar
And sit down to read the story of Sukhyang.

10

My mother-in-law bestows a gift:
A pair of jade boy pendants.
Without daring to speak a word
I tie them among my girdle tassels.

11

Through a chink in your window
I call softly, "Elder Brother!"
If longing for home were not forbidden
Tomorrow I would be sent off in a palanquin.

12

Taking up grass-green silk for yearning lovers
I use a pair of needles to put pockets on both sides.
I embroider three butterflies myself
And with my own hands I offer it to my husband.

13

Everyone enjoys playing on a swing;
I alone do not join in.
I insist that my arms are too weak to push,
But actually I'm afraid I'll lose my jade dragon hairpin.

14

I wrap it in a sun-patterned cloth
And store it in a bamboo chest.
At night I cut clothing for my husband;
Since my hands are fragrant, so are his clothes fragrant.

104　*Yi Ok*

Not only does she make her husband's clothes, but she raises the silkworms that spin the silk she will use to make them. The poem has indicated earlier that when she is sent off from her parents' home to join her groom's family, either out of shyness or more likely due to the strictures of Confucian regulation of contact between the sexes, she and her fiancé do not address each other for three months. Her love for him can only be expressed with her hands, although the poem does provide a touching moment when she addresses him as "elder brother" through a chink in his window; apparently not loudly enough to draw a response (or he dares not respond). The pair of jade boy pendants from her mother-in-law are an obvious reminder that the young woman's primary role in the family is giving birth to a son; the pendants are about her duty, not her desire to adorn herself. Even the jade hairpin she mentions is a reminder of her thrift; she refrains from participating in the recreation of the others because she fears losing it. Yi Ok does not, however, portray a young woman who thinks only of her duty. She is no one-dimensional representation of the ideal young wife. She longs for her husband and she misses her own family — she even puts her work down to read the story of Sukhyang, a fictive heroine abandoned as a baby who in the end is reunited with her family. Indeed, since the longing to speak to her husband and the longing for her family are described in the same stanza, they seem to be related. She has not yet established a true matrimonial bond with her husband, while the filial bond with her parents is already beyond her reach.

Yi Ok ends *The Song of Elegance* with an indication that the young woman is aware of how others mistakenly perceive her lot in life (Yi, 4, 285).

17.
人皆輕錦綉
儂重步兵衣
早田農夫鋤
貧家織女機

17
Everyone thinks it's easy to embroider,
But I also have to sew rough cotton cloth.
Early morning farmers hoe their fields;
In poor households women weave at their looms.

The young woman may be a paragon of love, respect, diligence and thriftiness — and Yi Ok certainly wants us to admire her — but he also grants her an awareness of how her station in life relates to the lives of others in late eighteenth-century Korea. This, I think, is what makes *Vulgar Maxims* extraordinary. The world of the poem is not all surfaces, textures and colors. It does not merely serve as a resource for the scholar of Joseon costume, for example, but allows for the complexity of the internal lives of those whose complexity has heretofore been elided. It isn't just that the young woman in *The Song of Elegance* is, well, a woman, but that she is the kind of woman whose thoughts have gone unrecorded in the sort of poetry considered valuable enough as literature to be preserved as such in language otherwise reserved for the most elevated of topics. Yi Ok not only recognizes that she actually has thoughts, but that they are complex and contradictory.

The wife in the second section, *Song of Splendor*, has a different relationship with make-up, clothing and accessories, but she, too, proves to be more complex than her adornment. Here are the first five stanzas (Yi, 4, 285–286):

18
莫種鬱陵桃
不及儂新粧
莫折渭城柳
不及儂眉長

19
歡言自酒家
儂言自娼家
如何汗衫上
臙脂染作花

20
白襪瓜子樣
休踏碧粧洞
時體針線婢
能不見嘲弄

21
頭上何所有
蝶飛雙節釵
足下何所有
花開金草鞋

106 *Yi Ok*

22
下裙紅杭羅
上裙藍方紗
琮琤行有聲
銀桃鬪香茄

18
Do not plant Ulleung peaches;
They cannot equal the freshness of my make-up.
Do not snap off branches of the Weicheng willow;
They cannot equal the freshness of my eyebrows.

19
You say, my love, you've come from a tavern;
I say you've come from a whorehouse.
Why is there sweat on your jacket
Blossom-streaked with rouge?

20
White stockings in the shape of wild rice stems
Do not step into the jade-adorned grotto.
Now I'm part of the thread-and-needle crowd,
Can I avoid being made fun of?

21
What's on my head?
A hairpin like a butterfly alighting on the knot of a bamboo
flute.
What's on my feet?
Blossoming flowers embroidered on my straw slippers.

22
My underskirt is of red Hangzhou gauze;
My overskirt is of deep blue satin.
Dangling jades tinkle whenever I walk:
Silver peaches contending with fragrant eggplants.

There is a delight, or merely just pride, in the details of make-up, dress and adornment that was absent from *Song of Elegance*. The "jade-adorned grotto" refers to the *gisaeng* entertainment district, which her husband apparently frequents and that she cannot enter. Unlike the newlywed of the previous section, this woman sees "the thread-and-needle crowd" to which she has been relegated, as something to be mocked. I also see an undercurrent of resentment at being confined to the home. Even as she obsessively describes how she is made-up, dressed and adorned, everything on her body is a reminder of the world beyond. Her make-up is the color of the peaches of a distant island, her eyebrows like willow branches from Weicheng (a reference to a famous poem of parting by Wang Wei (699–759)), her hairpin is like a butterfly, her slippers have embroidered flowers, her dangling jades are peaches and eggplants.

Yi Ok is not content to represent this woman as merely superficial. After all her reverie about her clothing is interrupted by a stanza in which she accuses her husband of having been to a whorehouse. If her adornment is intended to please her husband, it does not seem to have been entirely successful (Yi, 4, 286).

28
儂有盈箱衣
個個紫繡粧
最愛兒時着
蓮峰粉紅裳

29
三月松錦緞
五月廣月紗
湖南賣梳女
錯疑宰相家

28
I have a chest full of clothes,
All decorated with purple.
I most love those I wore as a child,
Clothes of Lotus Peak pink.

29
In the third month I wore pine gold satin;
In the fifth month I wore golden moon gauze.
A woman from Honam was selling combs;
She mistook me for the minister's wife.

Despite all her finery, the clothing she most loves is what she wore as a child. And the only person in the poem who appreciates her fine clothing seems to be a mere peddler woman far from home who mistakes me for a minister's wife. As Yi Ok points out in his brief introduction to Song of Splendor, it is about 驕奢浮薄夸飾 "pride

108 *Yi Ok*

and extravagance, frivolity and philandering, and exaggerated adornment." And yet, again, Yi Ok allows this woman a degree of self-awareness that spoils the pleasure she would otherwise take in the splendor of her appearance.

Yi Ok baldly explains that Section 3, *Song of Dissipation*, is about a 娼妓 "prostitute," not bothering to use a euphemistic turn of phrase to refer to her (Yi, 4, 287).

36
歡莫當儂髻
衣沾冬栢油
歡莫近儂唇
紅脂軟欲流

37
歡吸烟草來
手持東萊竹
未坐先奪藏
儂愛銀壽福

38
奪儂銀指環
解贈玉扇墜
金剛山畫扇
留欲更誰戲

36
My love, do not mess up my hair-do;
Camellia oil would stain my clothing.
My love, do not approach my lips;
My make-up would run down my face.

37
My love, if you come to me smoking,
I will take your Dongnae pipe.
Even before you sit down I will snatch it and hide it;
I love its silver inscriptions "long life" and "good fortune."

38
If you have come to seize my silver ring,
Reach deep into your purse to provide jade weights for my door panels.

Yi Ok 109

Diamond Mountain is painted on the door panels;
If you stay your desire, to whom will you next bequeath it?

I should first point out that there are no possessive pronouns in the original. Although I have added "my" seven times in stanza 36, in fact it may very well be the case that we should understand that the camellia-scented hair oil risks dripping onto the man's clothing rather than her own. Perhaps this is the woman who left rouge stains on the clothing of the husband of the woman in *Song of Splendor*. The ambiguity of the text in *hanmun* allows the reader to imagine that either the woman fears that he will spoil her clothing (and therefore she should remove it?), or that he risks staining his own clothing, or perhaps she merely wants an excuse to postpone his caresses and kisses until after she has been compensated. She intends to grab his pipe (what would Freud say?), pretending to admire the inscriptions but more likely intent on the value of their silver. Once she has encouraged him to reach deep into his purse, she cautions him about postponing his desire. Clothing and adornment clearly has a very different function in this section of the poem.

Later she is aware that a man whose name she does not know appears every night among the crowd of men who come to see and hear her perform (despite what Yi Ok has called her, she is obviously more than a mere prostitute). She does not know his name, nor does it seem to matter. She knows her place (Yi, 4, 288).

43
人言儂輩媒
儂輩實自貞
逐日稠坐中
明燭度五更

44
不知歡名字
何由誦職啣
挾袖惟捕校
紅衣定別監

43
People say we should get a matchmaker;
We are truly chaste.
Every day you are seated among the crowd;
A bright candle arrives at the fifth watch of the night.

110 *Yi Ok*

44
I don't know the gentleman's name;
Why recite an official title?
Everyone wearing narrow sleeves is an officer;
If you wear red, officials are infallible.

Since Yi Ok has called her a prostitute, she obviously is not chaste. Perhaps the other *gisaeng* have made fun of her for having an admirer who never approaches her and the resulting "chastity." As I've read this poem over and over, I've gradually come to suspect that the intimate encounter intimated at the beginning of *Song of Dissipation* may be imagined: "If you come to me, do not..." Or perhaps the physical encounter of the first stanza is a foil for the encounter that does not take place between the nameless admirer and the *gisaeng*.

In the final stanza of *Song of Dissipation* Yi Ok takes pains to acknowledge the self-awareness of the prostitute. Her performance does not end with a visit from the "chaste" admirer (Yi, 4, 288).

50
盤堆蕩平菜
席醉方文酒
幾處貧士妻
鎧飯不入口

50
Plates of mung bean jelly curd salad pile up;
The seated are drunk on *pangmun* wine.
How many places are reserved for the wives of poor scholars?
They don't even bother to eat the rice stuck to the pot!

The *Song of Dissipation* is not about her dissipation, but about the dissipation of her audience. In contrast to the thrifty bride who foregoes the pleasure of riding a swing for fear of losing her hairpin, the drunken men in the audience pay no attention to the food piling up around them. The third line is a rhetorical question, because of course there are no wives of any sort, let alone of poor scholars, in the *gisaeng*'s audience. The wife in *The Songs of Splendor* made it clear that she could never enter the *gisaeng*s' "jade-adorned grotto."

In the fourth and final section of *Vulgar Maxims*, the *Song of Inexpression*, Yi Ok lends his voice to a wife who complains that she is forbidden to voice her resentment. She does not speak about embroidery or make-up, but sewing, clothing and hairpins still inform her daily life (Yi, 4, 289–290).

57
三升新襪子
縫成轉嫌寬
箱中有紙本
何不照憑看

58
間我梳頭時
偷得玉簪兒
留固無用我
不識贈者誰

65
嫁時倩紅裙
留欲作壽衣
爲郎鬪篋倩
今朝淚賣歸

57
Three new pair of thick hemp stockings —
When I finish sewing them he starts to criticize.
In the suitcase is a paper pattern for making socks;
Why didn't I rely on it?

58
While I was brushing my hair
Someone stole my jade hair pin.
If I left it it's no use to me or
I do not know who I could have it given to.

65
An old red skirt from the time I was married off;
I've stopped wanting to make clothes for my old age.
In order to pay off all my husband's debts
This morning I weep as I sell off everything.

The wife in the final section of the poem seems to represent the new bride's marriage gone wrong. Instead of protecting her hairpin she's misplaced it (she retreats from the suggestion that someone has

112 *Yi Ok*

stolen it). The silence of the new bride's husband has given way to criticism. The detailed descriptions of clothing and their various fabrics are replaced with the blunt "an old red skirt." The wife here is weary of the world of objects that held the interest of the other three wives.

In my first reading of *Vulgar Maxims* I was put off by the obsessive detailing of archetypically female-associated objects, but now I think that Yi Ok manipulates clichés about women's lives to create four vivid, individual portraits. The recurrence of make-up, clothing and the damn hairpin give the reader some things to hold on to as he (and since the poem was written in *hanmum*, the intended reader must have been a man) moves through the lives of these four women who hold them in common. The restriction of the material world to this handful of things is a reminder of how circumscribed the experience of women was in late eighteenth-century Korea. There is a great deal more that could be said about Yi Ok's *Vulgar Maxims*, but I want to end his chapter with five stanzas that insist on shared experience across the diversity of women's marriages in late Joseon Korea (Yi, 4, 289).

51
寧爲寒家婢
莫作吏胥婦
纔歸巡邏頭
旋去破漏後

52
寧爲吏胥婦
莫作軍士妻
一年三百日
百日是空閨

53
寧爲軍士妻
莫作譯官婦
篋裏綾羅衣
那抵別離久

54
寧爲譯官婦
莫作商賈妻
半載湖南歸
今朝又關西

55

寧爲商賈妻
莫作蕩子婦
夜每何處去
今朝又使酒

51

I'd rather be the servant girl in a chilly house
Than the wife of a magistrate.
He's just left again to lead an inspection tour;
As soon as he fixes a leak he turns around to leave again.

52

I'd rather be the wife of a magistrate
Than the wife of a soldier.
In one year there are three hundred days,
But for a hundred of those the women's quarters are empty.

53

I'd rather be the wife of a soldier
Than the wife of a palace translator.
In the suitcase is clothing of damask and gauze,
Which is why the separation can go on and on.

54

I'd rather be the wife of a palace translator
Than the wife of a merchant.
After half a year he's returned from Honam
This morning he's already left again for Guanseo.

55

I'd rather be the wife of a merchant
Than the wife of a profligate.
Every night he goes somewhere else,
When he comes home in the morning he already sends out for
wine.

The universality of the sentiments expressed in these stanzas
grounded in the particulars of the late eighteenth-century Korean
woman's experience strikes me as the best argument of all for Yi
Ok's place in World Literature.

114   *Yi Ok*

Notes

1 For Korean terms, titles and citations from Yi Ok I will first give Chinese characters (which is what is found on the page), followed by *hangeul*, followed by transliteration of the *hangeul* (which represents how Koreans pronounce the characters) and finally the English translation.

2 Kim (2003, 258). Wall, Barbara and Lee Dong Myong. *Trauer über einen Schmetterling*. Thunum: Edition Peperkorn, 2010.

3 The literal meaning of 兩班 양반 *yangban* is "two ranks/classes/groups," referring to the division of government administrators into 文班 문반 *munban* and 武班 무반 *muban*, civil administrators and military officers. 文 and 武 are a classic yin-yang division (cultural and martial) dating back thousands of years in Chinese thought.

4 Kim Hŭnggyu translates Yi Oen as *Women's Songs*, but that is more a description than a translation (258).

5 The most famous Korean woman writer of the long eighteenth century (at least from the perspective of the early twenty-first century) was not a poet, but instead a memoirist, 헌경왕후 *Hoengyeong Wanghu* known as Lady Hyegyeong (1735–1816) to Euro-American readers. Married at a young age to Crown Prince Sado (1735–1762), her four memoirs relate in increasing detail court life of the mid-eighteenth century. Her husband never acceded to the throne. He seems to have gone insane. In order to rid himself of a problematic heir, his father King Yeonjo (1694–1776) had him locked inside a rice chest until he died of starvation eight days later.

6 Most of my information about Yi Ok's life comes from Youme Kim's dissertation *The Life and Works of Yi Ok*. To the best of my knowledge it is the only American dissertation ever written about Yi Ok.

Conclusion

The original title of this book, *Missed Readings: What's with World Literature*, was too clever by far and out of synch with how Routledge titles work. I nonetheless remain attached to the slippage from "missed readings" to "misreadings" implied by this title, because it is those readings that we miss which have led to the misreading of just what World Literature is or can be. Nicholas Rennie, a dear colleague in the Rutgers German Department, has helpfully suggested a title for the German translation: *Mistlektüre*. Despite the base meaning of "Mist," I would translate this as "stupid readings" rather than "shitty readings," which may well accord with the reaction of some readers, especially those unhinged by my displacement of Goethe from the axis of World Literature. This book has argued that professors who practice World Literature not only need to rededicate themselves to reading, but should also put to use their skills as critics, translators and teachers to explore just those readings that we have missed. As a corollary then, this book has asked practitioners of World Literature to think long and hard about why certain kinds of literary works remain excluded from consideration even as it goes about reading works gone astray, misplaced or overlooked, for World Literature is not a haphazard collection of texts that have struggled Darwinistically against each other to supersede their national traditions and survive in the arena of English translation. Professors have will and agency — World Literature is a responsibility of the individual professor, as scholar and teacher, to bring to the attention of his students and colleagues those works that they cannot read in the source language. Poems, plays, essays, novels and short stories, to name just a few genres of literature, that are not discussed and go unread are like misshelved books in a library (and lest anyone think that books can no longer go missing in this digital age, I have personally discovered two books labeled with the wrong title by Google Books). As David

116 *Conclusion*

Damrosch writes in his riposte to Emily Apter's trashing of the World Literature enterprise, *Against World Literature*, "The world is a large and various place" (Damrosch, 508). World Literature as currently practiced, however, risks shrinking that world into a small and monotonous place, grayed over by Theorization and metronomed by an unhealthy and distorting obsession with a handful of texts, pseudo-historical moments and critics.

As Theo D'haen points out in his essential *Routledge Concise History of World Literature*, differences between American and Western European practices of World Literature stem from their divergent locations (D'haen, 3). The source of World Literature in American universities is pedagogical, a result of the resistance to specialization that characterizes undergraduate education in the United States. In Western Europe, especially France and Germany, there is little impetus to think about *teaching* World Literature, so its practice is instead theoretical and research-driven. This is not to say that U.S.-based scholars do not theorize or conduct research on World Literature — this book itself is an example otherwise — but that the theorization of and research related to World Literature is informed by the question "What should we..." or "What can we teach our undergraduates?" This does not make us lesser scholars, sullied by contact with the world beyond the page, but instead serves as a reminder that while World Literature might be, in an ideal world, global, its practice is necessarily local.

I embrace the specificity of my task as a U.S.-based scholar and, although I am housed in a French Department, I do not suffer from unrequited love of all things French or wish that I could be more French or more German or more anything else in particular, despite my engagement with writers from various countries. So what then do I want a World Literature undergraduate to take away from a World Literature course (or a course informed by the practice of World Literature)? Since at my university it is altogether possible that any particular undergraduate will take but one literature course, I cannot hope to teach him all of World Literature, despite the ever-more-inclusive anthologies designed to help me achieve that ideal. Instead I want her to reach the end of the semester sensitized to complexity, diversity and difference, and to feel surprise, wonder and humility at the breadth and depth of human expression. I understand that "diversity" and "difference" (or, perhaps, *différance*) are buzz words in this profession, while the choice of "surprise" and "wonder" risks accusations of pandering to exoticism, so I will try to be more precise by pointing to recent books

Conclusion 117

in Comparative Literature that have fired up my World Literature cylinders before returning to this book and its argument.

Rebecca Gould's *Writers and Rebels: The Literature of Insurgency in the Caucusus* (Yale, 2016), Karen Thornber's *Empire of Texts in Motion: Chinese, Korean, and Taiwanese Transculturations of Japanese Literature* (Harvard-Yenjing, 2009) and Ronit Ricci's *Islam Translated* (Chicago, 2011) do not explicitly describe themselves as examples of the practice of World Literature, but for me they demonstrate what is both possible and necessary. It is probably not feasible for anyone to learn to read (let alone speak and write) Russian, Georgian, Chechen, Arabic, Turkish, Persian, Chinese, Korean, Japanese, Javanese, Malay and Tamil, the languages in play in these three books. Each of these books engages with an orbit of literary transmission, adaptation and translation that does not depend on English, French or German. The practice of World Literature has not always depended on exchange among Western European languages or, to be more blunt, translation into English. To pretend otherwise indicates blindness to our own critical and linguistic limits. The Caucasus of Gould's book is a nexus of local languages bordered by languages of greater reach (Russian, Turkish, Persian). Thornber's East Asia is a region of complex intercultural exchange bounded by millennia of Chinese cultural domination capped by the rapid rise of Japan as a locomotive of modernization at the end of the nineteenth century. In Ronit Ricci's South Asia and Southeast Asia are lands of overlapping Islamic texts where sources and genres blur into each other. These are worlds that World Literature has not had time for when constructing its paradigms, diagrams and theories. Our loss.

I do not want to imply that I am an exoticist nostalgic for days of yore when no Chechens bothered with English or the cosmopolitan Malay learned Arabic and Persian for access to worlds beyond his own. I worry, however, that if we remain as bound to the present as our students, worlds before global English will end up mere curios, little more than textual equivalents to eight-track tapes or land lines. What Aamir Mufti's *Forget English! Orientalisms and World Literatures* (Harvard, 2016) reminds us is that at the present moment English is not only the essential vehicle of World Literature, but that the emergence of World Literature is a result of the rise to dominance of English as a second language and the concomitant establishment of national literatures that have destroyed more complex "and sometimes ancient cultures of reading, writing, and performing" (Mufti, location 1934, Kindle). Where I part from Mufti is

118   *Conclusion*

his insistence that the "you" addressed by World Literature is necessarily Euro-American (Mufti, location 83, Kindle). Undergraduates in American universities are increasingly international, not from the idealistic desire of our administrators to increase diversity in the student population, but because foreign students generally pay full tuition and are therefore a source of revenue. That so many of my students are from China and Pakistan, for example, and so many of their parents are from Russia, Korea and Colombia, for example, means that I cannot assume a common knowledge of cultural references. For four decades literature scholars have decried centers, metropoles and hexagons, but our students have moved well beyond us. There is no center any more. Assuming the metropole is now foolhardy. I *can* assume that many of my students know things that I cannot — including languages, histories, songs and, yes, literary texts. Perhaps we should begin to think of the world in World Literature as starting with the students in our classes.

That world literatures before World Literature are receding into the misty past and world students are walking through the doors of our classrooms makes our task all the more urgent. I cannot force my students (or colleagues) to become polyglots in order to access a wider variety of literary works. They're busy. If Lawrence Venuti is right that "for most readers, translated texts constitute world literature" (Venuti, 192), then the relative paucity of works translated into English means that World Literature is by definition impoverished and skewed heavily toward works written in English (that English Departments tend to house World Literature courses only exacerbates the problem).[1] Where then are to be found the poetry by Chechen rebels, Japanese short stories in transnational motion, and the Malay adaptations of Persian devotional texts? In English or not — and here I differ with David Damrosch — they, too, belong to World Literature.

Reading in translation and teaching translated works have come in for some hard knocks in recent (and not so recent) years. In 2003, Gayatri Spivak criticized the assembling of anthologies of World Literature in English translation as certain to Americanize the reading of literature around the globe (Damrosch and Spivak, 2011, 456–457). Several years later Damrosch pointed out that for pecuniary reasons these anthologies were, in fact, available only in the United States, since American publishers refused to pay for the global rights of the assembled, translated texts (Damrosch and Spivak, 457). Although the specifics of Spivak's assertion were wrong (the *Norton Anthology of World Literature* in six volumes is not being forced on the Global South), it is nonetheless true that translations into English have an outsized influence on readership. The American market is the largest in the world, so it is no surprise that it affects what people outside the United States read. Emily Apter's *Against World Literature* (Verso, 2013) argues against what she sees as the ease with which all literature seems to slip into English, when scholars and teachers should insist on the untranslatability of texts from one language and one culture to the next. I do not disagree about the essential untranslatability of literary texts, although I would point out that one of the most untranslatable texts of all time, the Qur'ān, is also one of the most translated texts of all times. The problem is, unless we want our students and colleagues and ourselves to stick to English (and the other handful of languages that we may have managed to pick up along the way), we have no choice but to read at least some things and teach many things in translation. To me the solution is to read yet more things in translation — to translate more things, if one can, to question translations, to work with multiple translations when available.

Perhaps what Spivak, Apter and others mean to say is that our view of the world is necessarily skewed by the availability of works relatively easy to translate into English. I would push this further. It is not simply a question of whether a work can be translated easily or well into English, but whether it fits easily into categories of literature that the reader in English finds comfortable. It is far easier to teach a literary work that is recognizably a novel, a genre familiar to nearly everyone who reads English, than a work representing genres that have no counterpart in anglophone literature or that straddle genre boundaries that don't exist in its own tradition. In *Born Translated: The Contemporary Novel in an Age of World Literature* (Columbia, 2015), Rebecca Walkowitz, summarizing Doris Sommer, argues that "Particularist works are not meant to circulate globally. Rather, they are meant to be regional and to comment on the specific relationship among languages in that region" (Walkowitz, 33). My argument in this book has been that it is precisely these works that we need to research and teach, to read and translate; to exclude them from World Literature is about nothing other than avoiding the hard work of accounting for literary works and literary traditions that do not fall within the narrow categories established by scholars with insufficient language training (which would mean all of us; despite the continued dying-off of languages around the world, to understand the complexity of human experience requires acquiring more languages than any one person can master during his lifetime).

120 *Conclusion*

This is not to say that I expect all my colleagues to abandon Shakespeare, the novel or anything written in English because I want them to learn Amharic, scour the planet for under-researched genres and toil away at translation day in day out. The solution to the fear of the homogenization of literary culture, however, lies in seeking out, puzzling through and bringing to the attention of others literary works that have been missed or overlooked because they do not fit our notions of what literature is or how it works or what it does.

Note

1 David Bello lists seven major world languages (Swedish, Chinese, Hindi, Arabic, French, German and English) and quantifies book translations among them from 2000 to 2009. Eighty percent are from English into the target languages. Only 8% are into English, while 78% are into French or German (which means that World Literature should be taught in French and German rather than English). Adding Korean, Japanese and Russia would shift the statistics somewhat (French and German would be less dominant as languages of reception), while a recent uptick in translations into Chinese (especially from Arabic) would indicate some movement away from English as a pivot language. Nonetheless, the overall asymmetry would remain more or less the same (Bello, 203–204).

Bibliography

Amante, Adriana. "Echeverría, entre dos reescrituras." *Las ranas. Artes, ensayo y traducción* 2 (April, 2006), 3–10.

Badri, Taha Ibrahim Ahmed. "Friedrich Rückerts Beschäftigung mit der arabischen Literatur Motive und Nachwirkungen." *Languages and Translation* 25 (2013), 45–52.

Bobzin, Hartmut. "Friedrich Rückert und der Koran." *Der Koran in der Übersetzung von Friedrich Rückert*. Würzburg: Ergon Verlag, 2001, vii–xxxiii.

Borges, Jorge Luis. *Obras completas*. Buenos Aires: Empecé, 1996.

———. *Prólogo a El Matadero. Cuentistas argentinos*. Buenos Aires: Libresa, 2004. 126–127.

Bush, Christopher. "Reading and Difference: Image, Allegory and the Invention of Chinese." *From Sinographies: Writing China*. Ed. Haun Saussy, Eric Hayot, Steven G. Yao. Minneapolis: University of Minnesota Press, 2007. 34–63.

Carilla, Emilio. "Juan María Gutiérrez y *El Matadero*." *Anuario de Letras Lingüística y Philología* 32 (1994), 99–142.

Choi, Ji-Hee and Hong Na-Young. "The Costumes of 18th Century Joseon Dynasty from Lee Ok's Writings." *Journal of the Korean Society of Costume* 63.5 (August, 2013), 18–34.

Chow, Rey. *Writing Diaspora: Tactics of Intervention in Contemporary Cultural Studies*. Bloomington: Indiana University Press, 1993.

Claudel, Paul. *Le poète et le Shamisen*. Ed. Malicet, Michel. Besançon: Presses Universitaires de Franche-Comté, 1970.

———. *Connaissance de l'est*. Paris: Larousse, 1920.

Damrosch, David. "*Against World Literature: On the Politics of Untranslatability* by Emily Apter (review)." *Comparative Literature Studies* 51.03 (2014), 504–508.

———. *What is World Literature?* Princeton: Princeton University Press, 2003.

Damrosch, David and Gayatri Spivak. "Comparative Literature/World Literature. A Discussion of Gayatri Chakravorty Spivak and David Damrosch." *Comparative Literature Studies* 48.4 (2011), 455–485.

122   Bibliography

Echeverría, Esteban. *El Matadero. La Cautiva*. Ed. Leonor Fleming. Madrid: Ediciones Cátedra, 2009.

———. *El matadero: (The Slaughter House)*. Trans. Angel Flores. New York: Las Americas, 1959.

———. *The Slaughteryard*. Trans. Norman Thomas di Giovanni and Susan Ashe. London: The Friday Project, 2010.

Gabrieli, Francesco. "Ǧamīl al-'Udhrī. Studio Critico e Raccolta dei Frammenti." *Rivista degli studi orientali* 17 (1937), 40–71, 132–172.

Gamerro, Carlos. *Facundo o Martín Fierro. Los libros que inventaron la Argentina*. Buenos Aires: Sudamericana, 2015.

Gillespie, John K. "The Impact of Noh on Paul Claudel's Style of Playwriting." *Theatre Journal* 35.1 (1983), 58–73.

Gonzales Echevarría, Roberto. *Modern Latin American Literature. A Very Short Introduction*. Oxford: Oxford University Press, 2012.

Gutiérrez, Juan María. "Nota crítica a 'El Matadero.'" *El Matadero*. Buenos Aires: Instituto Distrital de las Artes, 2015. No pagination.

Haüßler, Sonja. "*Kyubang Kasa*. Women's Writings from the Late Chosŏn." *Creative Women of Korea. The Fifteenth through the Twentieth Centuries.* Ed. Kim-Reynaud Young-Key. London: Taylor & Francis, 2004. 142–162.

Hellerstein, Nina. "Écriture de l'exégèse, l'exégèse de l'écriture." *L'écriture de l'exégèse dans l'œuvre de Paul Claudel: actes du colloque les 8–9–10 mars 2001 à l'Université de Toulouse-Le-Mirail*. Besançon: Presses Universitaires de Franche-Comté, 2006. 283–298.

Iglesia, Cristina. "Echeverría entre dos siglos: las fundaciones de la crítica." *Cuadernos LIRICA* 10 (2014), 1–14.

Jitrik, Noé. "Between Being and Becoming. Identity, Latinity, and Discourse." *The Noé Jitrik Reader. Selected Essays on Latin American Literature*. Durham: Duke UP, 2005. 27–34.

———. "Forma y Significación en 'El Matadero' de Echeverría." *Suspender toda certeza: antología crítica (1959–1976): estudios sobre Cambaceres, José Hernández, Echeverría, Macedonio Fernández, Gabriel García Márquez, Roa Bastos, Donoso, Cortázar y otros*. Birlos, 1997. 65–96.

Johns, Anthony H. "A Humanistic Approach to *I'jāz* in the Qur'ān." *Journal of Qur'ānic Studies* 13.1 (2011), 79–99.

Kawakami, Akane. "Walking Underground: Two Francophone Flâneurs in Twenty-First Century Tokyo." *L'Esprit Créateur* 56.3 (Fall, 2016), 120–133.

Kim, Hŭnggyu. "Chosŏn poetry in Chinese." *A History of Korean Literature*. Cambridge: Cambridge University Press, 2003. 250–260.

Kim, Kichung. *An Introduction to Classical Korean Literature: From Hyangga to P'ansori*. London: Taylor & Francis, 1996.

Kim, Youme. *The Life and Works of Yi Ok*. PhD diss. University of California, Los Angeles, 2014. http://escholarship.org/uc/item/0g0576hz#page-70.

Loop, Jan. "Divine Poetry? Early Modern European Orientalists on the Beauty of the Koran." *Church History and Religious Culture* 89.4 (2009), 455–488.

Bibliography 123

Mani, Venkat. "Bibliomigrancy. Book Series and the Making of World Literature." *The Routledge Companion to World Literature.* Ed. Theo D'haen, David Damrosch and Djelal Kadir. London: Taylor & Francis, 2011. 283–295.

Mann, Susan. "Learned Women in the Eighteenth Century." *Engendering China. Women, Culture, and the State.* Ed. Christina K. Gilmartin, Gail Hershatter, Lisa Rofel, Tyrene White. Cambridge: Harvard University Press, 1994. 27–46.

———. *The Talented Women of the Zhang Family.* Berkeley, University of California Press, 2007.

Mayau, Catherine. "Claudel et la littérature japonaise ou Claudel en auteur japonais." *Paul Claudel et l'histoire littéraire: actes du colloque de l'Université de Paris-Est-Marne-la-Vallée (LISAA-EA 4120), de l'Université de Franche Comté (Centre Jacques-Petit-EA 3187), et de l'Université de Paris IV-Sorbonne (Littératures françaises du XXe siècle-EA 2577).* Besançon Presses Universitaires de Franche-Comté, 2010. 153–177.

Meng, Liuxi (Louis). *Poetry as Power. Yuan Mei's Female Disciple Qu Bingyun (1767–1810).* Lanham: Lexington, 2007.

Mercado, Juan Carlos. *Building a Nation. The Case of Echeverría.* Lanham: University Press of America, 1996.

Micciolo, Henri. *L'oiseau noir dans le soleil levant de Paul Claude: Introduction, variantes.* Presses Universitaires de Franche-Comté, 1981.

Nakano Shigeharu. "Paul Claudel." *Columbia Anthology of Modern Japanese Literature. Volume 1: From Restoration to Occupation, 1868–1945.* Trans. Myriam Silverberg. Ed. J. Thomas Rimer and Van C. Gessel. 606.

Nasr, Seyyed Hossein, Caner K. Dagli, Maria Massi Dakake, Joseph E.B. Lumbard, Mohammed Rustom, editors. *The Study Quran: A New Translation and Commentary.* HarperCollins. Kindle Edition.

Owen, Steven. "What Is World Poetry?" *The New Republic.* November 19, 1990, 28–32.

Paret, Rudi. *Der Korean. Übersetzung.* Eighth Edition. Stuttgart: Verlag W. Kohlhammer, 2001.

Quan Tangshi. Ed. Peng Dingqiu. Beijing: Zhonghua Shuju, 1960. Online version: http://ctext.org/quantangshi.

Rexroth, Kenneth. *Women Poets of China.* New York: New Directions, 1972.

Robertson, Maureen. "Voicing the Feminine: Constructions of the Gendered Subject in Lyric Poetry by Women of Medieval and Late Imperial China." *Late Imperial China* 13.1 (June, 1992), 63–110.

Rotker, Susana. *Captive Women. Oblivion and Memory in Argentina.* Trans. Jennifer French. Minneapolis: University of Minnesota Press, 2002.

Sagarra, Eda. "Friedrich Rückert's *Kindertotenlieder.*" *Representations of Childhood Death.* Ed. Gillian Avery, Kimberley Reynolds. London: Palgrave MacMillan, 2000. 154–168.

124 *Bibliography*

Schimmel, Annemarie. *Friedrich Rückert: Lebensbild und Einführung in sein Werk.* Göttingen: Wallstein Verlag, 2015. Kindle Edition.

Schmidt, Jerry Dean. *Harmony Garden. The Life, Literary Criticism, and Poetry of Yuan Mei (1716–1798).* London: Routledge/Curzon, 2003.

———. "Yuan Mei (1716–1798) on Women." *Late Imperial China* 29.2 (December, 2008), 129–185.

Sohn, Ho-Min and Lee, Peter H. "Language, Forms, Prosody, and Themes." *A History of Korean Literature.* Cambridge: Cambridge University Press, 2003, 15–51.

Sorensen Goodrich, Diana. *Facundo and the Construction of Argentine Culture.* Austin: The University of Texas Press, 1996.

Tarnopolsky, Noga. "Borges in the Afterlife." *New York Times Book Review.* August 22, 1999. www.nytimes.com/books/99/08/22/bookend/bookend.html.

The Columbia Anthology of Modern Japanese Literature. Ed. J. Thomas Rimer & Van C. Gessel. New York: Columbia University Press, 2013.

Thomas di Giovanni, Norman. "Introduction." *The Slaughteryard.* London: The Friday Project, 2010.

Tsu, Jing. "World Literature and National Literature." *The Routledge Companion to World Literature.* Ed. Theo D'haen, David Damrosch and Djelal Kadir. London: Taylor & Francis, 2011. 157–167.

Venuti, Lawrence. "Translation Studies and World Literature." *The Routledge Companion to World Literature.* London: Routledge, 2011. 180–193.

Von Grunebaum, Gustave Edmund. "I'djāz." *Encyclopaedia of Islam* 3 (1986), 1018–1020.

Walkowitz, Rebecca. *Born Translated. The Contemporary Novel in the Age of World Literature.* New York: Columbia, 2015.

Wall, Barbara and Lee Dong Myong. *Trauer über einen Schmetterling.* Thunum: Edition Peperkorn, 2010.

Wang, Yanning. *Reverie and Reality. Poetry on Travel by Late Imperial Chinese Women.* Lanham: Lexington, 2014.

Weipert, Bernhard. "Friedrich Rückert's Translation of the 'Hamāsa': Thoughts on its Present-Day Literary and Scholarly Value." *Quaderni di Studi Arabi* 8 (2013), 113–129.

Wieger, Léon. *Caractères chinois.* 3rd edition. Xianxian, China: Imprimerie de Hien-Hien, 1916.

Yi Ok. *Wanyoek Yi Ok Choenjip.* Seoul: Hyumoeniseuteu, 2009.

Yu, Anthony. "Biographical Note on and Translation of Sun Yunfeng." *Women Writers of Traditional China. An Anthology of Poetry and Criticism.* Ed. Chang, Kang-i Sun and Haun Saussy. Stanford: Stanford University Press, 1999. 562–564.

Yuan Mei. *Suiyuan Nüdizi Shixuan in Yuanmei Quanji.* Ed. Wang Yingzhi. Nanjing: Jiangsu Guji Chubanshe, 1993.

Yuefu Shiji from *Sibu Congkan.* Shanghai: Commercial Press, 1919–1936. Vol. 1954–1969.

Index

Note: Page numbers followed by "n" denote endnotes.

Abū Tammām 81
Against World Literature
(Apter) 119
Ahmed, Shahab 91n2
al-Akhṭal 66
Algerian Literature 2
Alter, Robert: *The Art of Biblical
Poetry* 91n3
Amalia (Mármol) 52
Amharic language 78, 120
"Ancient Feelings" 20–21, 23, 24
anecdote 66–68, 70–73, 75,
76, 76n2
anthologization 6
*Anthology of Poetry by the Female
Disciples of Harmony Garden*
(Yuan Mei) 11
Apter, Emily: *Against World
Literature* 116, 119
Arabic Literature 61, 62, 66, 67, 76,
80, 82
Arabic poetry 2, 84, 86
Arab tradition of lyric poetry 61
Arberry, A.J. 92n7
Argentine Literature 45, 47, 49–55
The Art of Biblical Poetry (Alter)
91n3
Ascent to the Temple of Concealed
Brilliance 16–17
The August Sleepwalker (Bei Dao) 38

Badri, Taha 91n5
Baidu 41
"Ballad of Mulan" 22–23
Baudelaire, Charles 46–47

Bei Dao 28, 37, 39–44, 44n2, 48;
The August Sleepwalker 38
Bello, David 120n1
Birth of a Nation (Griffith) 60
Bobzin, Hartmut 87, 89
Bo Juyi 17, 21; Empress's Quarters
18–19; Lodging Alone at
Transcendent Journey Temple
17–18
Book of Songs 61–76
"Borges and I" (Borges) 48
Borges, Jorge Luis 47–49, 55;
"Borges and I" 48; "Cult of the
Phoenix" 48; "El Aleph" 49;
"Pierre Menard, el autor del
Quijote" 49; "The Garden
of Forking Paths" 48, 49;
"The Library of Babel" 48
*Born Translated: The Contemporary
Novel in an Age of World
Literature* (Walkowitz) 119

Camus, Albert: *The Stranger* 46
Cao Xueqin 8
Carilla, Emilio 55
cassical Chinese poetry 42
Cervantes 46, 47, 49
Cheng Tingmao 9
Chinese architecture 35
Chinese character 31–33, 35–37, 43,
93; figural theory of 30; Korean
pronunciation of 94
Chinese landscape poetry 14
Chinese Literature 5–6
Chinese poetry 7, 9, 28, 38–40, 100

126 Index

Chinese writing system 31, 36
Chow, Rey 28, 37, 39–40; *Rey Chow Reader* 28; *Writing Diaspora: Tactics of Intervention in Contemporary Cultural Studies* 28
classical Arabic poetry 66, 84
classical Chinese poetry 10, 11, 39, 41
The Classic of Poetry 9, 100, 101
Claudel, Paul 2, 25–44
Columbia Anthology of Modern Japanese Literature 27
Comparative Literature 1, 2, 117
Complaining of Love (Li Bo) 19
Confucian temple 33, 35
contemporary Chinese poetry 28, 39, 43
Contemporary Civilization (CC) 60n1
couplet 11, 13–15, 20, 21, 42
Crown Prince Sado 114n5
"Cult of the Phoenix" (Borges) 48

Damrosch, David 5, 24, 40–44, 115–116, 118; *Longman Anthology* 8; *World Literature in Theory* 81
Daneri, Carlos Argentino 49
Dante Alighieri 44
Dawn Walk 14–15
Descartes, René 60n1
D'haen, Theo: *Routledge Concise History of World Literature* 116
dīwān 61–62
Djebbar, Assia 2
Dostoevsky, Fyodor Mikhailovich 47
Dream of the Red Chamber 8, 24
Du Fu 18
Du Mu 15; Mountain Journey 16

Echevarría, Gonzales 57
Echeverría, Esteban 3; "El Matadero" 52, 54–55, 57; *La Cautiva* 45–60
Eckermann, Johann Peter 55
"El Aleph" (Borges) 49
"El Matadero" (Echeverría) 52, 54–55, 57
Emperor Qin 101

Empire of Texts in Motion: Chinese, Korean, and Taiwanese Transculturations of Japanese Literature (Thornber) 117
Empress's Quarters (Bo Juyi) 18–19
Encyclopaedia of Islam (Von Grunebaum) 91n1
English language 3, 80
English Literature 80
Essays (Montaigne) 46
Euro-American Literatures 67
Euro-American readers 31

Facundo o civilización y barbarie en las pampas argentinas (Sarmiento) 51
Fanon, Frantz 60n1
Finkel, Donald 42, 43, 44n2
Finnegans Wake 6
Fleischer, Heinrich 83, 84, 89
Floating on Ruoye Creek in Spring (Qiwu Qian) 15–16
Fong, Grace 7
Forget English! Orientalisms and World Literatures (Mufti) 117
The Fortunate Union 56
Foucault, Michel 60n1
Francophone Literature 46; scholarship 2
Frankenstein 62
French Literature 26, 46
French poetry 47
Freytag, Georg: *Lexicon Arabico-Latinum* 82

Gabrieli, Francesco 61, 62, 68, 81
Gamerro, Carlos 50–51
García Marquez, Gabriel 47
"The Garden of Forking Paths" (Borges) 48, 49
generalization 4, 33, 57
German Literature 80, 81
Germanophone Literature 46
German Qur'ān 87, 90
Goethe, Johann Wolfgang von 3, 46, 55, 56, 80, 81, 91, 115; *Sorrows of Young Werther* or *Faust* 81
Goldziher, Ignác 80

Index 127

Golius, Jacob 82
Gould, Rebecca 117;
  Writers and Rebels: The
  Literature of Insurgency in the
  Caucusus 117
Great Works 45, 46
Griffith, D.W.: *Birth of a Nation* 60
Gu Cheng 42–43
Gutiérrez, Juan María 50, 54–55

ḥadīth 67, 76n2, 84
Ḥamāsa 81
Hammer-Purgstall, Josef von 83,
  84, 86
hangeul 93, 99, 114n1
hanmun 98, 100, 101, 109
Hebrew language 78
Hernández, José: *Martín Fierro* 51
Himmel, Annemarie 80
Hispanophone Literature 46
Huckleberry Finn 6

Ibn Qutayba 91n1
Iglesia, Cristina 57
Invitation to French Poetry
  (Dover) 27
al-Isfahānī, Abū al-Faraj 3, 66
Islam 67, 82, 91n2
Islam Translated (Ricci) 117

Jade Terrace Collection
  (Quan Deyu) 21
Jamīl Buthayna 61–76
Jeong Yakyong 97
Jing Tsu 56
Jitrik, Noé 54, 60n3
Johns, A.H. 91n1
A Journey 12–13
Joyce, James 44

Kabuki 27
kadhdhaba 88
Kindertotenlieder 81
King James Bible 80, 91n3
King Jeongjo 98
King Sejong the Great 93
Kitāb al-Aghānī (Book of Songs) 61
Knowing the East (Lawler)
  27–28, 37

Ko, Dorothy 7
Korean Literature 94, 95
Korean Mystery Detective Jeong
  Yakyong 97
Korean poetry 93

La Cautiva (Echeverría) 45–60
Lady Hyegyeong 114n5
Lawler, James: *Knowing the East*
  27–28
Legge, James 28–29
Les Misérables 46
Les Miz 46
Lexicon Arabico-Latinum
  (Freytag) 82
Li Bo 18, 21; Complaining of
  Love 19
"The Library of Babel" (Borges) 48
Literature Humanities (Lit Hum)
  45–47
Lodging Alone at Transcendent
  Journey Temple (Bo Juyi) 17–18
Longman Anthology (Damrosch) 8
Loop, Jan 83, 91n5
Lugones, Leopoldo 51
lyrical language *(jabān al-janān)* 74
lyric poetry, Arab tradition of 61

Madama Butterfly 60
McDougall, Bonnie S. 38, 42, 44n2
Mahler, Gustav 81
Mani, B. Venkat 91n4
Mann, Susan 7
Manon Lescaut (Prévost) 57
Mansilla, Eduarda 50
Mansilla, Lucio 50
Mármol, José: *Amalia* 52
Martín Fierro (Hernández) 51
modern Chinese poetry 28, 42, 43
Modern *Japanese* Literature 25
Molière 60n1
Montaigne, Michel de 47, 60n1;
  Essays 46
Mountain Journey (Du Mu)
  13–14, 16
Mufti, Aamir: *Forget English!*
  Orientalisms and World
  Literatures 117
The Music Bureau 100

128 *Index*

Nakano Shigeharu 3, 25, 44n1
national literature 6
neo-Confucian canon 97
Neuwirth, Angelika 80
The New Republic 38, 39
New Yorker 48
Nöldeke, Theodor 80
non-Muslim Euro-Americans 91n2
non-Muslim non-Arabophone
    reader 77, 78

Obras completas 55
Orientalism (Said) 37
"Oriental" languages 80
Owen, Steven 28, 37–41, 43, 48

Palace Poem (Xue Feng) 19–20
Paret, Rudi 82, 92n7
Philippe, Charles-Louis 27
"Pierre Menard, el autor del
    Quijote,"(Borges) 49
Pound, Ezra 30, 43
Prévost, Abbé 57; *Manon
    Lescaut* 57
Pride and Prejudice 47
Prophet Muḥammad 62, 66, 67, 72,
    79, 82

Qing Literature 7
Qing travel poetry 12
qiṣṣa 73–75
Qiwu Qian 15; Floating on Ruoye
    Creek in Spring 15–16
Quan Deyu: *Jade Terrace
    Collection* 21
Qu Bingyun 8
Qur'ān 6, 67, 77–92, 119
Qur'ānic Arabic 90

Rabelais, François 60n1
Racine, Jean 46
Realism 54
"Religion of the Sign" 29, 37
Revista del Río de la Plata 55
Rexroth, Kenneth: *Women Poets of
    China* 24n1
The Rey Chow Reader
    (Chow) 28, 40
Ricci, Ronit: *Islam Translated* 117
Riefenstal, Leni: *Triumph des
    Willens* 59–60

Rioplatense Spanish 54
Rolland, Romain 26–27
Rotker, Susana 60n4
Rousseau, Jean-Jacques 60n1
*Routledge Companion to World
    Literature* 81
*Routledge Concise History of World
    Literature* (D'haen) 116
Rückert, Friedrich 3, 77–92

Saer, Juan José 52
Said, Edward: *Orientalism* 37
Sarmiento, Domingo Faustino 52;
    *Facundo o civilización y barbarie
    en las pampas argentinas* 51
Schimmel, Annemarie 82
Semitic languages 78
Shakespeare, William 44, 46, 120
Sichuan 17
Silverberg, Miriam 25, 44n1
Sommer, Doris 119
Song of Dissipation 108–110
The Song of Elegance 104–105
Song of Inexpression 110–113
The Song of Splendor 105–108, 110
Sorrows of Young Werther or *Faust*
    (Goethe) 81
Spivak, Gayatri 2, 118, 119
The Stranger (Camus) 46
sui generis genre 77
Sun Yunfeng 3, 5–24
Sūrat al-Raḥmān 84–86

al-Ṭabarī 89
Tang poetry 7, 15, 17, 19, 24, 24n3
The Temple of Concealed
    Brilliance 17
theorization 4, 36, 116
Thornber, Karen 117; *Empire of
    Texts in Motion: Chinese, Korean,
    and Taiwanese Transculturations
    of Japanese Literature* 117
1001 Nights 6
Time 27
Toqueville, Alexis de 60n1
traditional Chinese etymologies 31
travel poetry 10, 12, 14, 15, 24
Triumph des Willens (Riefenstal)
    59–60
Tsu, Jing 91n4
al-Tustarī 89

Index   129

Udhrī 62
Ulmann, Lion 83
*Une Promenade à travers la
    littérature japonaise* 29
Unnachahmlich 77–92

Valéry, Paul 27
Venuti, Lawrence 118
verkennen 88, 90
"vernacular Chinese" 39
Voltaire 60n1
Von Grunebaum, G.E.:
    Encyclopaedia of Islam 91n1
Vulgar Maxims 95, 105, 110, 112

Wahhābī Islam 91n2
Walkowitz, Rebecca: *Born
    Translated: The Contemporary
    Novel in an Age of World
    Literature* 119
Wang, Yanning 12
"The Web" 48
Widmer, Ellen 7
Wieger, Léon 28, 29;
    figural theory of Chinese
    characters 30
Women Poets of China
    (Rexroth) 24n1
*Women Writers of Traditional
    China: An Anthology of Poetry
    and Criticism* (1999) 8
Woolf, Virginia 45

World Literature 1–8, 15, 24, 25, 27,
    28, 40, 41, 44, 45, 48, 55, 59–61,
    70, 76, 79, 80, 91, 93, 94, 113,
    115, 117, 118
World Literature (Apter) 116
World Literature in Theory
    (Damrosch) 81
World Poetry 38, 43
World Poetry 28
*Writers and Rebels: The Literature
    of Insurgency in the Caucusus*
    (Gould) 117
*Writing Diaspora: Tactics of
    Intervention in Contemporary
    Cultural Studies* (Chow) 28

xï 21
Xue Feng: Palace Poem 19–20

*Yale Anthology of Modern French
    Poetry* (Mary Ann Caws) 27
yangban 114n3
Yi Ok 3, 93–114
Yi Sang 84
Youme Kim 114n6
Yuan (1271–1368) Literature 7
Yuan Mei 6, 7, 9, 10; *Anthology of
    Poetry by the Female Disciples of
    Harmony Garden* 11
Yuefu Shiji 24n4

Zhu Xi 101

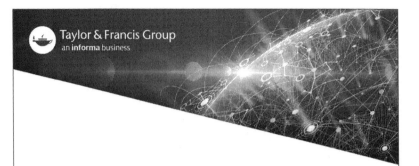